MW00328859

Sheila has painted a picture of e. .... who is ready to trust God. She has shown us that it's not necessarily the headliners who make the difference in our world. It's you and I taking small steps of obedience and trust, believing that God will use those steps for His purposes. Those little mustard-seed steps can have a tremendous impact in God's world. I pray that after reading this book, you will have newfound courage to act on God's convictions! You ARE somebody, and you can with I AM!

Duane Matz
Going Home Show Host, The Family, WEMI Radio

Sheila Luck has written a touching and entertaining guide to enhancing your faith life. Where most books provide vague aspirations, Sheila's provides concrete ways to grow in faith and increase your spirituality. By giving "real life" examples, the reader is shown a path that anyone can follow.

Thomas A. Carroll
CFA

I would highly recommend this book to any Christian looking for those challenges, opportunities, and blessings to enhance their Christian walk.

Kathy L. King
Retired Corporate Librarian and Records Manager

I Can with I AM is a valuable resource to be used over and over again as your life changes and evolves. This book is written in a way that pertains to everyone's daily lives.

Gary and Linda Madsen
Retirees

I Can with I Am is one of the most inspirational books that I have read in a while. Doing what we can in our everyday life to serve others and God is a very underplayed concept in a society that only thinks of themselves. Sheila Luck captures your heart with very personal heartwarming and convicting stories of love and sacrifice. Even if you don't think that you need to read a book like this, trust me ... you do! You will walk away with a renewed vision of God's plan and purpose for your life!

Doreen Shirek
Chapter Director with Wisconsin Right to Life
Pastor's wife and Women's Ministry Director of Faith Christian Church in Mauston, WI

In *I Can with I Am*, Ms. Luck clarifies that real human significance is to be found in knowing and serving Christ and one another. She suggests not confusing hours spent in church pews with time spent in relationship with Jesus, and coins the memorable phrase "love others out loud" to stress that our caring must be visible and real wherever and whenever situations arise. The author shares her life experiences vulnerably and suggests readers practice transparency as well. Forgiveness for past sins like abortion is spoken about simply and powerfully. She motivates readers to a deeper awareness of their life mission. *I Can with I Am – Be Somebody* conveys important truth that can transform lives and ultimately the world.

Dr. Judith Rolfs
Author of *Never Tomorrow*

I Can with I AM – Be Somebody is a powerful and insightful read into the heart and soul of a woman who lost her way, but found healing, love, and purpose in Christ. The story is told by intertwining personal examples with biblical stories, a unique perspective which will guide readers into evaluating and changing their own lives.

Barbara Lyons
Retired Executive Director of Wisconsin Right to Life

I CAN
with
I AM

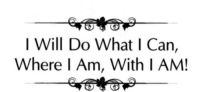

I Will Do What I Can,
Where I Am, With I AM!

I CAN
with
I AM

BE "SOMEBODY!"

SHEILA M. LUCK

ANEKO
PRESS

Printed in the United States of America

Aneko Press – *Our Readers Matter*™

www.anekopress.com

Aneko Press, Life Sentence Publishing, and our logos are trademarks of

Life Sentence Publishing, Inc.

203 E. Birch Street

P.O. Box 652

Abbotsford, WI 54405

RELIGION / Christian Life / Inspirational

Paperback ISBN: 978-1-62245-417-4

eBook ISBN: 978-1-62245-418-1

10 9 8 7 6 5 4 3 2 1

Available where books are sold

Contents

For our daughters and their husbands, with love.

I am only one,
But I am one.
I cannot do everything, but I can do something.
And I will not let what I cannot do
Interfere with what I can do.
—Edward Everett Hale

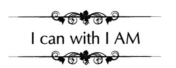

I can with I AM

Acknowledgements

So many people have been instrumental in the writing of this book. It would not be the product it is without them.

First, as always, my husband's support and encouragement is a necessary ingredient in all my books. He allows me to work at my own pace, listens to my struggles, and provides ideas when I seek his advice.

Our daughters are always willing to listen. And I really appreciate their input when I have questions on whether they and others their age will relate to the issues I raise. Oh, if I could only think like a twenty-six-year-old. They help to keep my thoughts young.

Next, there are my faithful friends. How can I thank them enough for their help?

Colleen Hansen read every one of my manuscripts, more than once, to provide gentle but honest feedback. She says things like, "This chapter would make more sense to me if it were in this other location. I'm not sure what your point is in this section. Have you considered combining these two chapters? Maybe it's just me, but I was very confused when I got to this section." I'm certain that it wasn't just Colleen. She's a very bright woman. If she's confused by something I've written, then I've written something that is confusing. Thank you, Colleen.

My friend Mary Vandenberg probably felt like an owl as she repeatedly tried to teach me to use the word "who" instead of the word "that." "Who, who, and who" was written frequently in the margins, as she freely offered her time to provide an initial edit of my early manuscript. One would think that by age fifty-eight and into my sixth book, I would have better grammatical skills. Maybe I should have taken more English and writing classes in college. Thank you, Mary, for your edits, patience, and teaching skills.

Pastor Duane Matz critiqued this book to ensure I used Bible verses and references correctly from a theological perspective. He also provided numerous suggestions of additional verses, stronger verses, and biblical accounts, which helped bring the many concepts to life. Pastor Duane, thank you.

A number of friends agreed to read the manuscript and provide words of endorsement, some after further editing. These include Kathy King, Tom Carroll, Barbara Lyons, Tom Boyle, and more. The back cover is only big enough for a few endorsements, but I'm grateful for websites and Facebook. There, I can post additional comments and endorsements. Thank you all for taking time from your busy schedules to read this manuscript. (If any new readers would like to share a comment, my contact information can be found on my website: *www.sheilaluck.com.* I'd love to hear from you.)

Finally, but never to be viewed as less important, I thank everyone at Aneko Press. You are all so talented, thorough, creative, and thoughtful. I love how each of you maintained your focus on God first. Your suggestions have been solid, presented with grace while listening to my questions and concerns. Thank you. May God continue to bless each of you and your work.

I will close this section with the most important

acknowledgement of all. Jesus said, *"I am the vine; you are the branches. If you remain in me and I in you, you will bear much fruit; apart from me you can do nothing"* (John 15:5). Thank you, Lord Jesus, for placing this work upon my heart, for blessing me with the opportunity and desire to complete this work, and for your endless patience as I repeatedly allowed busyness to interfere with progress.

Jesus is the Vine. With him, I can make a difference, a real difference. With God, I am not only one. With the Great I AM, I can do more than something. I can, with I AM, make a difference, a real difference, and so can you.

Introduction

For most of my life, beginning in my very early years, I wanted to be "somebody." I wanted to be a person others looked up to, a person others believed was bright, wise, and filled with potential. I wanted to be respected and perhaps admired by others. I wanted to be somebody important, somebody successful.

I didn't really know what an important person looked like or acted like. I had never identified with any role models. So I didn't have a specific plan or direction. In high school, I thought that to be somebody, you had to be popular. So I wanted the popular kids as my friends. I also noticed that it helped someone become popular if they were good in sports. I tried volleyball and basketball but had limited talent for sports that required hand-eye coordination. But I was fast. I could run, so I went out for track. In an effort to be somebody, I held a class office, participated in the art club, and worked hard on my grades.

By the end of high school, I believed that to be somebody, money was important. So I pursued a college degree in a field I thought would bring me the best income in the shortest period of time. I graduated and took a job as an engineer in an era when engineering wasn't a typical field for women. As I achieved each new step, I discovered that there was always a more successful person out there. I wasn't the somebody I had dreamed of. So I went to law school, graduated, and found fantastic employment for a major oil company. The pay was good. I received promotions, and thought I was well on the path to being somebody.

It sounds good, doesn't it? Maybe it depends on your definition of *somebody*. God had been telling me for many years that my definition of *somebody* wasn't his definition, but I didn't really hear him. I didn't understand his message. I wanted with all my heart to be somebody. I became the somebody I thought I wanted to be, but God had a different plan.

Money, career, and material success do not define a person as somebody. Those things might be gifted to you, but think about Solomon. He asked God for wisdom so he could properly lead as king of the Israelites. God blessed Solomon with wisdom and gifted to him many riches. The wealth did not turn Solomon into somebody. Solomon became somebody due to his wisdom. Even today, he is known as the wisest man of all time.

My friends and family tease me about my creative ideas to solve life's many problems. Ever since I was in high school, or maybe even earlier, I would see a problem, come up with a solution, and say, "Somebody should do that." Then I would do nothing.

Somebody should do that. Why doesn't somebody fix that? If only somebody would intervene, the problem would be solved. Have you ever asked, "Why doesn't somebody do something?"

Maybe I was supposed to be the somebody who made a difference. If only I had followed through on one of my many ideas. It's possible that when God put those many ideas and solutions in my mind and in my heart, he was trying to open a door for me to be the somebody who made a difference.

In Christ, God has made us *all* somebody. He brought us

into his family. We are God's children. We are men and women of God and princes and princesses of the King of Kings. Simply by our faith in Jesus Christ, we are somebody. But it doesn't end there. With God, the Great I AM, we can become somebody by the way we live. We can make a real difference in the world around us. We can be the somebody that does it, fixes it, changes it, resolves the problem, makes things better, influences positive change, helps our neighbors, or makes a difference.

Through Christ, we are somebody. With him, we can become somebody. When we align our lives with God, the Great I AM, and act in accordance with his will, we will succeed. It's a sure thing.

Isn't that awesome?

Each and every one of us can be somebody. Each and every one of us can, with I AM, do all things which he has called us to do without bounds. Through God, in Christ, our potential is limitless. We can with I AM. With God, we can make a difference and impact this world and his kingdom in a positive way.

Each of us has the ability to start right now and waste no more time.

I pray this book helps you understand how to draw close enough to God to hear him whisper in your ear and allow him to lovingly guide you into his world and the plan he has for you. God has a plan for your life. In his plan, you possess amazing potential. With him, the Great I AM, you can realize your God-given potential.

Discover the possibilities. Be somebody. Commit to doing what you can. *I will do what I can, where I am, with I AM. I can, with I AM, be somebody.*

You can with I AM.

Chapter 1

I AM

I will do what I can, where I am, with I AM.

My name is Sheila. I've never been fond of my name, because I wasn't sure it fit me. As I matured and became comfortable in my own skin, I still didn't know if my name was a fit. I own a coffee cup that has my name and its supposed meaning printed on it. According to this "trusted source," my name means "dream maker." It says, in part, "You help out when others don't know what to do. With imagination you make dreams come true." According to another source, the name *Sheila* means that I'm idealistic and generous, with a passion to improve the conditions of humanity and to serve others. I like that meaning. That's the kind of person I'd like to be. In fact, my personal and business mission statement is to help others find their God-given potential to be the somebody that God wants them to be. Maybe my name is a fit after all.

Does a name make a person or help others understand who you are? Does a name matter?

The Bible is replete with mentions of names, and it gives specific reasons or meanings behind the names. *Adam named his wife Eve, because she would become the mother of all the living* (Genesis 3:20). When Hagar was pregnant, an angel came to her and told her to name her son Ishmael, explaining that God had heard her misery (Genesis 16:11). The name *Ishmael* means "God hears." When God declared to Abram that he would be the father of many nations, God changed Abram's name to Abraham, which means "father of many" (Genesis 17:5). At the same time, God changed the name of Abraham's wife from Sarai to Sarah. He promised to make her the mother of nations and that kings would come from her line (Genesis 17:15-16). In Genesis 32, Jacob wrestled with a man all night. At dawn, the man requested that Jacob let him go. Jacob refused to let him go without a blessing. *Then the man said, "Your name will no longer be Jacob, but Israel, because you have struggled with God and with humans and have overcome"* (Genesis 32:28).

I will do what I can, where I am, with I AM. Who is I AM?

God said his name was I AM when he appeared to Moses through a burning bush and called him to go to Egypt to free the Israelites from centuries of slavery and oppression. Moses argued with God. He didn't believe he was capable. Specifically, he questioned what he should answer if anyone asked who sent him.

> *God said to Moses, "I AM WHO I AM. This is what you are to say to the Israelites: 'I AM has sent me to you.'"* God also said to Moses, *"Say to the Israelites, 'The LORD, the God of your fathers—the God of Abraham, the God of Isaac and the God of Jacob—has sent me to you.' "This is my name forever, the name you shall call me from generation to generation."* (Exodus 3:14-15)

I AM is God, the God of Abraham, Isaac, and Jacob.

What does *I AM* mean? What can we learn about God from this name? The baby name books don't list *I AM* as a name. But the Bible contains many descriptions of God. Perhaps the description in Revelation 11:17 is the best fit. When the seventh trumpet sounded, many heavenly voices declared that the kingdoms of the world were now the kingdoms of Christ and that he will reign forever. The twenty-four elders, who sat before God, declared in worship, *"We give You thanks, O Lord God Almighty, The One who is and who was and who is to come, Because You have taken Your great power and reigned"* (Revelation 11:17 NKJV).I AM is the one who is, the one who was, and the one who is to come. I AM is the Alpha and the Omega.

"I am the Alpha and the Omega," says the Lord God, *"who is, and who was, and who is to come, the Almighty"* (Revelation 1:8). God was God from the beginning, is God today, and will be God forever. God is I AM now and forever.

> *Before me no god was formed, nor will there be one after me.* (Isaiah 43:10b)

I will do what I can, where I am, with God, the one and only God, the Alpha and the Omega, God from the beginning, God of today, and God everlasting.

I Will Do What I Can, Where I Am, With I AM!

Chapter 2

The Plan of the Great I AM

"For I know the plans I have for you," declares the LORD, "plans to prosper you and not to harm you, plans to give you hope and a future." (Jeremiah 29:11)

Many are the plans in a person's heart, but it is the LORD's purpose that prevails. (Proverbs 19:21)

In their hearts humans plan their course, but the LORD establishes their steps. (Proverbs 16:9)

God, the Great I AM, sets the plans.

We often want to know the plans God has for us and try to look far into the future wondering what the end point might be. Some people plan for retirement or for when their children are grown and move into homes of their own. Others only plan for the week, for tomorrow, or perhaps for just that afternoon.

From a planning perspective, common job interview questions include: Where do you see yourself in five years? What is your career plan?

Our daughter Chelsy, when she applied for a job at a YMCA, was asked, "Where do you see yourself in five years?"

She responded, "I don't know. God hasn't told me yet."

She didn't get the job. But was she right in that response?

Some might say, "No, because she didn't get the job."

I say, "Yes."

Maybe she could have said, "I will follow God and let him lead. I don't yet know his plans, but I'll be ready. In the meantime, day by day, I will do what I can, where I am, with I AM." I like that answer. But that answer probably wouldn't have landed her the job either.

Perhaps she could have said something like, "I'm trying to build my skills through work and educational experiences so that I will be able to _____ [fill in the blank]. I believe such experience will also prepare me for other opportunities in case God has a different plan for my life."

Chelsy knew God had a plan for her and intended to respond in accordance with his plan for her life. Until she understands his plan for her, she does what she can each day.

I often see things that need to be done, but usually the things I see are too big for me. Additionally, I often see grand-scale solutions. I usually follow up my thoughts with statements like, "If I had a ton of money, here's how we could fix this problem. Or, if I managed our government, I'd start to fix the debt problem by removing the government from all services that can be adequately provided through private sector employment."

Then, after I've told someone my self-declared, brilliant solution, I drop it. Why? Didn't I believe it was a good solution? I almost always believe my ideas are good solutions. My husband could tell you, "She always thinks she's right." However, I haven't thought through the implementation of my plans. I haven't identified step one, let alone steps two through fifty. I neither thought about step one, nor have I tried to take step one.

I'll do what I can. Instead of dreaming up all kinds of solutions to the problems I encounter with no follow-through, perhaps I will try to *do* something. I will start by doing what I can where I am. It sounds like a simple first step. *What I can* is something I can do today, with the time, materials, and skills I have today. It is step one. Maybe if I take step one, step two will become apparent, and the means to accomplish step two will become available.

> *"Whoever can be trusted with very little can also be trusted with much, and whoever is dishonest with very little will also be dishonest with much."*
> (Luke 16:10)

"Wait a minute," you say. "That's not an effective way to get anything accomplished." Stephen Covey, in his book, *The 7 Habits of Highly Effective People*, advises to "begin with the end in mind" and then create the plan. So you, dear Sheila, are wrong. To take one step, without a plan, without the end in mind, won't get you to the place where you need to go.

Okay. Planning is a good idea. However, when we work in and for God's kingdom, whose plan are we pursuing? Are we supposed to create the plan or let God create the plan? God is the Great I AM. God is the one in charge. He's been in charge since the beginning of all time. He's God, after all. God said that he has a plan. So, who am I to say to God, "Here is *my* plan. Will you bless it?" even though my husband is correct when he says, "She always thinks she's right."

> *A person may think their own ways are right, but the LORD weighs the heart.* (Proverbs 21:2)

So, is Stephen Covey wrong when he says that we should begin with the end in mind? No, he's not wrong either. But with whose end are we beginning? Am I to begin with *my* end goal, my vision? Or am I to begin with God's end goal, his vision?

The answer should be obvious. Because God is God, he's the one with the vision. It's his plan that counts, no matter how many plans I make. I may *think* I'm always right, but I *know* God is always right.

Those of you who work for companies and businesses in the United States will commonly find that the company or business has a vision statement, a mission statement, and a three- or five-year business plan filled with business goals or steps along the way. If the goals are met, they will bring the company closer to the realization of its vision. If I work for such a company, I will be directed to pursue my work in such a way as to meet the goals laid out in the business plan. The company's vision, mission, and goals form the foundation for my daily work.

Yes, the company has an end in mind, and it wants me to pursue that end in how I do my work, so each goal can be met. Unless I'm in top management or am the owner of the company, I don't get to define the goals or the vision. I simply follow along, join the corporate team, and work toward the vision by reaching the corporate goals that are within my personal world of work.

But notice in this corporate example, I don't define the goals or the vision. The owner, president, or CEO of the company defines the mission, and my supervisor defines my goals. I simply agree to participate when I accept the job. I choose to follow, join, and pursue the goals and plans set by those in charge.

Now, let's return to God and the concept of *doing what I can*. God is the one in charge. He sets the plan. If I want, I can choose to be part of his organization and work with him and for him to reach his goal, his plan, and his vision.

Sometimes, I might know God's greater vision, or I might only know an immediate goal. I might only know a step that I can do.

Why doesn't God tell us the whole plan? I don't know.

The major oil company I worked for early in my employment

career used a phrase as part of their confidentiality policy that limited disclosure of certain information to only those who had a "need to know." On occasion, I believe God discloses his plan, whether all or part of it, to us on a "need-to-know" basis. Our response requires faith and obedience.

For example, when God told Abram to move from his home in Haran, God said that he would bless him, and that all families would be blessed through him. God gave to Abram his vision but didn't tell Abram precisely where he was to move. Instead, God simply asked Abram to go to the land that he would show to him. God sought obedience, and Abram responded in faith and with obedience. Abram had all of the information he needed to know. All he needed to know was God's command (Genesis 12:1-4).

Abram's faith never fails to astonish me. I find it difficult to picture myself packing up and moving my family to another location without a plan, a job lined up, or even a particular direction in mind.

Often, we want to know all the details before we take a step forward. We want to understand the entire plan and know the reason or purpose for God's direction. This is particularly true when God's call doesn't seem to make sense to us. As with Abram, our faith is tested, and God asks us to step forward in obedience without knowing the end goal, without understanding the plan or purpose, and without reason that matches our own understanding.

We don't always understand God's plan or purpose.

Did you ever use or hear the statement, "Because I said so"?

"But why should I do that?" a teenager will ask.

"Because I said so," his mom responds, tired of the constant questioning of her requests.

Once in a while, she asks for simple obedience.

"Don't ask so many questions. Just do what I ask you to do."

Maybe God isn't ready to tell you why. Maybe God doesn't *want* to tell you why. And maybe he knows that you wouldn't understand his reasons at this point in time, so he simply asks you to obey.

> *"For my thoughts are not your thoughts, neither are your ways my ways," declares the* LORD. *"As the heavens are higher than the earth, so are my ways higher than your ways and my thoughts than your thoughts."* (Isaiah 55:8-9)

"Yes, Lord. I will do what I can," is the only correct response.

Sometimes, what I can do is nothing more than a simple first step, and I don't know where it might lead. In fact, I don't *know* that the first step is actually a step toward anything at all. Maybe by doing what I can, where I am, with the Great I AM, I will meet his goal intended to be met through me for today. Period.

What shall we do? We should do what Joshua said in Joshua 24:15: *"But as for me and my household, we will serve the* LORD.*"* I don't know what you're going to do, but I'm going to serve the Lord. I will do what I can, where I am, with I AM.

Will you commit to the same? Will you do what you can, where you "am," with I AM? Let's dig deeper before you commit. Such a commitment should not be made lightly.

I Will Do What I Can, Where I Am, With I AM!

Chapter 3

Who Can Refuse?

I dug into my files the other day and discovered my Last Will and Testament. My husband has a nearly identical will. We wrote them about ten years ago, so I hardly remembered what they said. Since that time, our children have become adults, we moved to a different home, we belong to a new church, and we found new favorite charities. Because of all these changes, it's time to revise our wills and update them to better reflect what we would want done with our money, property, and any sentimental items if we should die today or in the near future.

My Last Will and Testament might be considered my final wishes regarding my stuff, money, and property. But I'm quite certain that if I faced impending death and knew my life would be coming to an end sooner rather than later, I wouldn't be worried about my stuff, money, or property. To manage those things in advance is helpful to those who survive me and are saddled with difficult decisions. But I wouldn't give such items the elevated status of being my dying wish, my most heartfelt desires, or the deepest concerns of my heart.

My dying wishes would stem first from my love for my

husband and children. I would ask my husband to continue to find strength in the Lord, to always be available to our daughters, and to listen to them with an open heart. Additionally, I'd ask him to find new companionship, someone special with whom to share each day. I'd encourage our daughters to do similarly, to find strength and love in Christ first, then in their husbands, and finally in their children (if they should have children). I would ask them to support each other and their dad, and encourage them to honor God in all of their relationships with others as God places specific people in their lives. Finally, I would ask my sister and sisters-in-law to try to draw close to our daughters and be there for them if they should ever need a motherly heart to advise or console them. Even though our daughters are now adults, I don't think a woman ever fully outgrows her need for a motherly heart to turn to from time to time.

If I'm blessed to be able to say these things just prior to my death in this world, I picture myself pleading with my husband, our daughters, my sister, and sisters-in-law, "Will you do these things? Will you promise? Say that you will. Say, 'I will.'" I would insist on and seek their promises.

At the end of the day, I can only imagine an affirmative response. "I will. I promise," would be their reassuring words, a vow from each and every one of them. With those words, their promises, I would find comfort in my last moments of life on this earth.

Imagine this. Someone you love dearly is dying. His days on this earth are clearly numbered. With only a few last words of love, he makes a final request. Out of concern for his family members, his loved ones, he asks you to be available with a loving heart. He asks you to show love toward all those he loves. His eyes plead with you. All the while, you both know his death is coming in days, maybe even in hours. What do you say? How do you respond? Could you say anything other than yes?

"Yes. Of course I will. I will love those you love and show them your love so they never forget you. Through the love I share with them, all those you love will always know your love and remember you."

Would that be your answer? Would you say, "Yes, I will"? Be careful with your answer. Consider the cost when you make a promise, this promise. It sounds like an easy promise to make, but what counts is the follow-through, not the promise alone.

> *Whatever your lips utter you must be sure to do,*
> *because you made your vow freely to the* Lord *your*
> *God with your own mouth.* (Deuteronomy 23:23)

Now, what if Jesus was the person who faced death in days or hours? Would such a promise made in response to Jesus' dying request be a promise you would keep? Can you imagine his words voiced shortly before his crucifixion? Can you picture his eyes filled with love and pain at the same time? How would you respond to *his* dying request?

We *know* Jesus' final request. He asked for me. He asked for you. He asked for our love.

It was the evening before Jesus' crucifixion. He knew his time on earth as a man was coming to an end, and he washed his disciples' feet. He shared a meal with them, which included bread and wine. Then he explained that those elements represented his body broken for them and his blood shed for them. He asked his disciples to follow his example when they shared bread and wine in the future to remember him. Finally, Jesus foretold Judas's betrayal and his own crucifixion.

This was the last evening Jesus would be alone with his disciples. It was his final opportunity to speak to his twelve disciples privately and to pray privately to his Father in heaven. This was his last opportunity to privately present his dying requests.

To the disciples, Jesus spoke warnings of things to come

and gave them a new commandment, saying, *Love one another. As I have loved you, so you must love one another* (John 13:34). He also asked them to remain in his love and noted that they would do this if they kept his commands, in the same way that he remained in God by keeping God's commands (John 15:9-17). Jesus, in his last words to his disciples on their final evening alone, asked his disciples to remain in his love by keeping his commands and, specifically, by loving one another.

The biblical account doesn't describe precisely how the disciples responded. However, it's clear that Jesus' words confused them. They didn't understand that he would be crucified the next day on the cross. They didn't know the words he spoke were his final words and dying requests to them.

Then, as told in John 17, Jesus prayed to his Father in heaven. In this prayer, he again voiced his final requests, his remaining heartfelt wishes. First, he prayed that God would be glorified through his death. Then, he prayed for his disciples and asked the Father to protect and sanctify them. Finally, he prayed for all people who believed in him, both then and in the future. Jesus prayed for us.

> *"My prayer is not for [my disciples] alone. I pray also for those who will believe in me through their message, that all of them may be one, Father, just as you are in me and I am in you. May they also be in us so that the world may believe that you have sent me. I have given them the glory that you gave me, that they may be one as we are one—I in them and you in me—so that they may be brought to complete unity. Then the world will know that you sent me and have loved them even as you have loved me."*
> (John 17:20-23)

It is here that Jesus prayed for unity between all believers and the Father, between all believers and Jesus, and between all believers and each other.

What is unity? Oneness.

Unity is when there is such a close relationship that it's difficult, if not impossible, to distinguish the separate beings. There is unity when separate things are combined to form one. A union can be formed by persons, beings, things, thoughts, or positions.

Unity can be likened to a jigsaw puzzle. Once assembled, the puzzle pieces form a single picture. Each piece works in conjunction with the others to form a seamless whole. Oneness. Unity.

Imagine two people as they dance together in a waltz, salsa, or even the Texas two-step. One person leads and the other follows. The leader communicates subtly but clearly to the follower through gentle touch, a shift in weight, or slight pressure or movement of his hand. His distinctive movements are perceived by the follower, who responds almost instantaneously. Their individual steps and responses flow together as though they are one person. They dance in seamless unison. Oneness. Unity.

Couples who have been married for several years often blend together in unity. One completes the sentences of the other. They seem to talk without words. A mere glance communicates volumes from one person to the other. Oneness. Unity.

God the Father, God the Son, and God the Holy Spirit are God, one God. There is only one God. The three share the same name. As Jesus said, *Therefore go and make disciples of all nations, baptizing them in the name of the Father and of the Son and of the Holy Spirit* (Matthew 28:19). Jesus said to baptize in the *name* of the Father, Son, and Holy Spirit, not to baptize in the *names* of the Father, Son, and Holy Spirit. There is only one name and only one God. There is unity between the Father, Son, and Holy Spirit.

The Son lives and acts in complete unity with the Father.

Jesus was there with God, he was God, right from the beginning. John 1:1 states, *In the beginning was the Word, and the Word was with God, and the Word was God.* The Word is Jesus. Jesus was with God right from the start. Jesus is God. Both Jesus and God were together when all of creation was made.

> *The Son is the image of the invisible God, the first-born over all creation. For in him all things were created: things in heaven and on earth, visible and invisible, whether thrones or powers or rulers or authorities; all things have been created through him and for him. He is before all things, and in him all things hold together.* (Colossians 1:15-17)

To know God, we need just to look at Jesus. Do you want to know what's important to God or what breaks his heart? Do you want to know if God cares about the difficulties you face in life, or if he cares about the joyous occasions in our lives? Study the Gospels – the first four books of the New Testament – and you will know Jesus.

Know Jesus and you will also know God. *No one has ever seen God. But the unique One, who is himself God, is near to the Father's heart. He has revealed God to us* (John 1:18 NLT). Jesus is God; he is in close relationship with God. Jesus is in perfect unity with God.

> *Philip said, "Lord, show us the Father and that will be enough for us."*
>
> *Jesus answered: "Don't you know me, Philip, even after I have been among you such a long time? Anyone who has seen me has seen the Father."* (John 14:8-9a)

Not only is Jesus in perfect unity with God, but so too is the Holy Spirit.

The Spirit was with God at the time of creation. *Now the earth was formless and empty, darkness was over the surface of the deep, and the Spirit of God was hovering over the waters* (Genesis 1:2). All creation was made with unity between the Father, Son, and Holy Spirit.

The Spirit was also present at the time of Jesus' baptism. *As soon as Jesus was baptized, he went up out of the water. At that moment heaven was opened, and he saw the Spirit of God descending like a dove and alighting on him* (Matthew 3:16).

Of course, simply being present or participating in an activity doesn't equal being in unity. However, the Spirit knows God's mind, his thoughts. *For who knows a person's thoughts except their own spirit within them? In the same way no one knows the thoughts of God except the Spirit of God* (1 Corinthians 2:11).

The Holy Spirit is also in unity with Jesus, just as Jesus is in unity with God the Father. We know this, because Jesus told his disciples that when the Holy Spirit, or Counselor, came, he would remind them of everything Jesus told them (John 14:26). To remind them of everything Jesus told them, the Spirit would have to be in unity with Jesus. Like Jesus, the Spirit says only what he hears. What he hears comes from Jesus, and what Jesus says is from the Father. Perfect unity.

> *But when he, the Spirit of truth, comes, he will guide you into all the truth. He will not speak on his own; he will speak only what he hears, and he will tell you what is yet to come. He will glorify me because it is from me that he will receive what he will make known to you. All that belongs to the Father is mine. That is why I said the Spirit will receive from me what he will make known to you.* (John 16:13-15)

What Jesus has, does, and says comes from God the Father. Jesus does only what he sees the Father doing. The Spirit says only what he hears from Jesus. Therefore, the Holy Spirit can say only what the Father says. And the Spirit knows the mind of the Father because he is God's own Spirit. The three, God the Father, God the Son, and God the Holy Spirit are one God. They are one. They act and speak in perfect unity.

Here's the exciting part. Jesus prayed, as his final request and dying wish, that we, as believers, would live in unity with him just as he lives in perfect unity with the Father. Jesus wants all believers – us – to live in him, and for him to live in us, in total unity. If we live in unity with Jesus, we will be able to hear Jesus, see what the Father does, and listen to the Spirit as he tells us what is on the mind of God. We will know our God-given potential as we live our lives through him, in him, and with him. In unity with Jesus, we will be somebody. Just imagine the possibilities.

Maybe you're thinking, *I want to live in unity with Christ but don't know how to do it.* The answer starts in 1 John 4:16b. *Whoever lives in love lives in God, and God in them.* If we live in love, God lives in us. If God lives in us, Jesus does also, because Jesus is in unity with God. Jesus lives in us, just as God lives in us, and just as God's love lives in us. Thus, Jesus prayed that God's love in us would bring unity among us. When we dwell in God's love and express his love to others, we live in unity with God the Father, God the Son, and God the Holy Spirit. Through this love, we also live in unity with all other believers. This love and unity in our lives becomes the fulfillment of Jesus' prayer, the evidence that Jesus is the Messiah.

> *By this everyone will know that you are my disciples,*
> *if you love one another.* (John 13:35)

The crux of this portion of Jesus' prayer in the Garden of Gethsemane – in which he prayed for unity between all believers and between them and God (See John 17:20-23) – was that all people of this world will know that he is the Messiah. Jesus wants all people of this world to be saved. Through Jesus' prayer, he asked all believers to live in unity with him and live lives of love. By doing so, we are invited and enabled to participate in God's plan of salvation for all people.

As we demonstrate God's love, all people will know that Jesus is Lord. This is *the* impact, the greatest impact, that those who believe in Christ can make. As we pursue oneness with God, our potential is limitless, and the positive impact we make on the world around us is without bounds.

> *Dear friends, since God so loved us, we also ought to love one another. No one has ever seen God; but if we love one another, God lives in us and his love is made complete in us.* (1 John 4:11-12)

Will you seek unity with God? Will you share God's love with all those around you? Will you do what you can with the Great I AM? Will you say, "Yes, I will do what I can where I am, with I AM."

I Will Do What I Can, Where I Am, With I AM!

Chapter 4

Living in Christ

W hen I left my day job in an effort to respond to God's call on my life, I entered a new world, a somewhat religious world in which I was unfamiliar with the fine details. I use the word *religious* intentionally here to mean religion rather than faith. In an effort to fit in, I tried to speak in such a way that others with more spiritual experience or maturity would find acceptable.

I didn't adjust my personal testimony or faith itself. But I attempted to conform in my procedure, protocol, and practices. In my early years as an attorney, I learned basic practices, such as how to follow the proper protocol to address other attorneys in written correspondence, as compared to addressing a judge, court commissioner, or patent examiner. I learned when to use *Sir* or *Your Honor*. When I closed a letter, I found myself forced to choose whether *Sincerely*, *Best regards*, or *Very truly yours* best reflected my business sentiments. I learned to use the correct margins on my documents, when to double space my lines, and when to use single-spaced lines when I filed certain court documents or patent applications. I needed to know the procedural rules that applied to my work.

The form and procedure mattered.

So, when I changed gears in my mid-forties to write and speak in the Christian world, I suddenly discovered that I didn't know the form, procedure, or protocol when communicating with others. Again, I found myself wondering about the proper way to close a letter. I looked to others' letters to see if there was a standard closing.

Some used *Blessings*. Others used *May God be with you*, which has become one of my personal favorites. Some stayed with traditional letter closings such as *Sincerely* or *Best regards*. Then I noticed some used *In Christ*.

Hmm, I thought. *That has a nice ring. I wonder what it means. I think I'm "in Christ,"* I said to myself, *but I'm not really sure I know what it means.* Well, even though I wasn't certain I understood what it meant, I started to close my letters and emails with *In Christ,* because I believed that I was, in fact, living *in Christ*.

When I looked up the word *in* on my laptop look-up feature in Microsoft Word, I found a definition from the Encarta Dictionary: English (North America) that says the core meaning of the word *in* indicates that *something or somebody is within or inside something*.

When I think about me being inside Jesus, or Jesus inside me, I picture such closeness or nearness that one is, in fact, in the other's heart and soul. To be *in* or *within* Christ, I see that I have to be so close to Jesus that he lives in me, my heart, my soul, and my entire spiritual being. Unity. Oneness. In Christ.

> *This is how we know that we live in him and he in*
> *us: He has given us of his Spirit. And we have seen*
> *and testify that the Father has sent his Son to be the*
> *Savior of the world. If anyone acknowledges that*

*Jesus is the Son of God, God lives in them and they
in God.* (1 John 4:13-15)

Raised in a Christian denominational church, I was baptized
as an infant in accordance with their tradition, attended con-
firmation classes, and affirmed my baptism upon completion
of those classes. I wandered a bit and then returned to church
after marriage. My husband and I chose to raise our children
in the same tradition and have been members of a church near
our home ever since. We only changed church membership
when we changed homes.

In spite of all that church-going, I didn't understand the
concept of a relationship with the Lord until I was thirty-eight
years old. It wasn't until then that I answered his call upon my
heart. I acknowledged that I am a sinner in need of a Savior,
and truly recognized and accepted Jesus as my Savior, he who
died on the cross and rose again. I was thirty-eight years old
when my life had a new beginning in Christ, when I took my
first real steps in relationship with Jesus.

Here's the real kicker. Until that time, I didn't know what I
was missing. In fact, I didn't know that I was missing anything
at all. But until that time, I wasn't living *in* Christ. I just went
through the motions. In my mind, I knew Jesus and his love,
but that love had not travelled the long path from my mind to
my heart.

"What happened?" you ask.

I experienced something unbelievable, nothing short of
miraculous. It was so simple that I had no idea what an impact
it would have on my life from that point forward.

I attended a women's retreat sponsored by my sister's
church. I really didn't want to go. The pace of my life already
consumed me, and it was hard for me to imagine giving up an
entire weekend for a women's retreat. I didn't really like that
kind of thing. But out of love for my sister, I agreed. *I can't turn*

her down every year, and this is important to her, I thought. *I hope I don't have to sit around and do crafts. I'm not into crafts.*

We *were* presented with opportunities to do crafts, but we didn't have to participate in that part. Thank goodness. Just because I'm a woman doesn't mean I like to do crafty projects. I'd rather read, research, study, attend seminars, and learn. Oddly enough, that's fun for me. To each his own, or her own.

Fortunately, for me, the retreat was filled with learning opportunities coupled with worship, music, skits, and excellent speakers. There were serious moments of prayer, conversation, and presentations sprinkled with a touch of humor and comic relief. The weekend offered content to stimulate the mind, coupled with opportunities to connect with the heart.

It started Friday night and ended after Sunday worship, with an afternoon break on Saturday. My sister and I used the break productively for lunch and shopping. Although the retreat events captured my attention, so much time focused on God and faith packed into a single weekend overwhelmed me, a person who thought one hour on Sunday morning was a sufficient allocation of time for God. So after our short shopping break Saturday afternoon, I considered telling my sister that I wanted to skip the Saturday night session. I was getting church-stuff burnout.

I was tired. I had had enough … or so I thought. But once again, not wanting to disappoint my sister, I went with the flow and attended the Saturday night session with her.

It was then, near the end of that session, that it happened.

The worship leader began to pray. She invited all to pray with her and asked us to join her in prayer if we wanted Jesus to be in our lives. She extended the invitation for anyone who wished to pray with someone personally to come up front where many prayer leaders waited.

I really didn't want to walk up front to pray. But sure, I wanted

Jesus in my life. *Hey, I go to church. We take our daughters to church. We've been going for a number of years now. Of course I want Jesus in my life. He's already part of my life, isn't he?* The thoughts ran through my head as I prayed with the worship leader from my seat in the crowd. (Did I mention there were a thousand women at this particular retreat?)

We prayed words of praise and thanksgiving, words that acknowledged Jesus as Lord, and as our Savior. The words became mine as I prayed that I was a sinner in need of a Savior, in need of Jesus. I asked him into my heart and into my life. I don't recall what words I used specifically. As we continued to pray, I felt the Lord, through the Spirit of God, enter – yes, I said enter – my heart. My chest felt as though it would burst as Jesus moved in and my old self was forced out.

I didn't know what it meant or what was happening. Under different circumstances, my symptoms could have caused me to believe I was experiencing a heart attack or some other serious health condition. But *this* evening, I knew it wasn't something physically bad, but rather something spiritually great. Jesus was in me, and I was in him, a condition (one might say) that was terminal – terminal to my old self. My experience shared more in common with a heart transplant than a heart attack. I received a new heart, a new life. I was *in* Christ and he was *in* me.

So that's what John described in John 4:13-15. He gave me his Spirit. I testified that Jesus was the Son of God and the Savior of the world, *my* Savior. Through that testimony, that faith, that belief, and a simple request for a Savior, Jesus moved into my heart. He lives in me and I live in him.

It was nothing short of miraculous. Yet it was so simple. I merely had to ask.

I now know why I was drawn to the words *In Christ* as my closing in written correspondence. I am *in Christ*.

I'm not sure why I was so surprised. As a young girl, the

church we attended had a picture on the wall which depicted Jesus knocking at a door. The door had no handle or knob on the outside. It implied that Jesus wouldn't enter unless someone opened the door from the other side and invited him in. This is a very well-known picture of Jesus. My grandmother explained it to me. She said the door represented the door to our hearts. Jesus wants us to invite him into our lives and into our hearts. So he knocks until we open the door.

The point of the picture, its message, isn't the artist's creation. Rather, the artist created his visual interpretation of Revelation 3:20. There, the Bible tells us that Jesus will knock at the door, and he makes a promise. *If anyone hears my voice and opens the door, I will come in and eat with that person, and they with me.* This Bible verse says that we simply need to open the door. Jesus is waiting for an invitation into our lives.

Although I knew who Jesus was since I was a child and I believed in him, I didn't understand what others meant when they said they had a relationship with Jesus until I opened the door at that women's retreat. I opened the door as I prayed and I invited Jesus to eat with me, to live in relationship with me.

I could have invited Jesus into my life at any time. I didn't need to be at the women's retreat or have the worship leader lead us in prayer. I didn't need to be in church. I just needed to make the invitation. Jesus was waiting at the door and knocking. I had ignored him for so many years.

Have you heard Jesus knock at the door of your heart? Perhaps you didn't know he was there, or maybe you just weren't listening. Maybe you've never seen nor understood that painting or didn't know about that verse from the book of Revelation. The reason doesn't really matter. If you haven't invited Jesus into your life, I encourage you to do so. If you want to live in Christ and want him to live in you, if you want a new life, I invite you to pray with me now:

Dear Lord Jesus, Son of the Father, Son of God. You came to earth, were born as a baby, lived as a man, and died on the cross, all out of love for me, a sinner. I have sinned in many ways, ways that I recognize, recall, and regret, and ways I don't yet realize or understand. I am a slave to sin and in need of a Savior from my sins. You, dear Jesus, through your death on the cross and your resurrection, have paid the price for me and my sins. I ask you to enter my life, enter my heart, guide my soul, and give me new life, a life in you through your Holy Spirit. I ask that you be my Savior. I thank you, dear Lord Jesus, for your sacrifice. Your love overwhelms me. Through you, in you, and with the help of your Holy Spirit, enable me to honor you with my life. In loving relationship, I pray in your holy name. Come, Lord Jesus. Amen.

This is how we know that we live in him and he in us: He has given us of his Spirit. And we have seen and testify that the Father has sent his Son to be the Savior of the world. (1 John 4:13-14)

To ask Christ into your life and accept him as your personal Savior is a wonderful start to a full relationship with him. However, a relationship takes much more than a one-time conversation through prayer. You must draw near to God and seek him daily. When you do, he will respond and draw near to you (James 4:8).

I will seek him today and always. Through God's Spirit, I will live in Christ, in unity with him. In Christ, I can make a difference. In Christ, I am somebody, and as somebody, I will do what I can, where I am, with I AM.

I Will Do What I Can, Where I Am, With I AM!

Chapter 5

Living in God's Love

Why does Jesus knock? Why does he want to live in me, in you, or in the heart of your neighbor? Why does he wait at the door of our hearts? He is in unity with God the Father, the God above all gods, and Jesus is God. Why did he pray for unity with us, mere humans, as his final request?

I'm just me. I wake up in the morning with bed head and mascara smudged beneath my eyes. I spill when I eat and can be a total klutz at times. I make mistakes and regret some things I've done, things I'd prefer to keep secret.

Why does Jesus wait at my door and love me, when I'm so imperfect and even a little icky at times?

Why? Because he loves us, whether we think we're loveable or not. Jesus loves the unlovable. Through him, we all become loveable. He covers all of our weaknesses, mistakes, and sins. Even when we've done what seems unforgivable, we are loved.

My heart breaks for the mom or dad who gets a phone call in the middle of the night. "Mr. and Mrs. Jones, we need you to come to the police station. We have your son here." Upon arrival, they learn their adult son has killed their daughter-in-law in a fit of rage. She was the mother of their two grandchildren. They learn that her parents have just left the hospital with the grandchildren. They wonder what will happen to them, who will take care of them, and whether they will get to see their grandchildren ever again. Their own son, a young man they love dearly, has done the unthinkable.

Later, they have to read about it in the newspaper. His picture is on television for all to see. The hurt, pain, worry, and embarrassment is unbearable. Relentless reporters call their home and knock on their door. These parents just want to be left alone as they search for a solution to their horrendous situation.

Their son committed the unthinkable, the unforgivable. Their son … can they ever forgive him? Their love seems shattered. When their shock wears off, anger overcomes them, and they lash out with words of hatred directed toward their own son.

In shock. Hurt. Angry. Are they unlovable?

I think of the son. My heart also goes out to him.

He's not sure how rage got the best of him, and he sits in his cell overwhelmed by guilt. The future he pictured for himself is gone. He loved her and hated her. His thoughts turn to their children. How can he ever explain to them what he did, or why, when he doesn't even understand it himself? He didn't plan it. He didn't intend to kill her. His anger blinded him to the point that he didn't know what he was doing.

Separated from the rest of the world by steel bars, he sobs and concludes that he's dirt, scum, the worst of the worse. He wishes he were dead. His parents' words replay in his mind, words of anger, sadness, and disappointment. And he agrees with them but doesn't know what to do about it. He hates himself and believes he is unloved and unlovable.

Ashamed. Guilty. Is he unlovable?

What about his children? What feelings of guilt will they carry? Will they wonder if they played a role in the situation?

If we hadn't been fighting when Dad got home ... I should have never told Dad about that phone call, but I didn't know it would make him so mad. I should have shoveled the snow when Mom asked. Then Dad wouldn't have blamed Mom. I should have ... I shouldn't have ... If only ... All of it was my fault!

At fault? Guilty? Are the children unlovable?

Do you feel unlovable? Have you done something in your life that seems unforgivable?

I have. And I felt unlovable because of what I did. I tried to escape from choices made in my youth and hoped that if I ignored them, I could overcome them. If I kept my choices hidden and kept them as a lifelong secret, I thought no one would know. No one needed to know. If they didn't know, they couldn't condemn me for my actions and my ultimate choice.

My ultimate choice wasn't an act of rage like the actions of the son. Instead, I acted out of loneliness and fear. The decisions I made led to the death of my unborn baby. Those decisions began with an unhealthy search for love and ended in an unplanned pregnancy and abortion.

Fortunately, for me, our society doesn't plaster my photo on the front page of the paper for committing murder. But my heart knows that I chose to take the life of my own child. The weapon used was the equipment housed in a so-called medical clinic. The procedure was one that our current society tries to hide under the guise of women's health care, a woman's right to reproductive choice.

For nearly thirty years, I tried to run from the guilt and hide my choice from all who knew me. The guilt turned to self-incrimination and shame. Then it adversely affected my personality, self-esteem, and overall well-being. I lived in the aftermath of the unthinkable. Do my mistakes and regrettable choices make me unlovable?

When I kept silent, my bones wasted away through
my groaning all day long. (Psalm 32:3)

Does rejection by others make us unlovable?

Many of us, although we want to be loved, often feel unlovable due to something other people have done to us or around us. For some of us, it's as simple as wanting to be married, but a potential marriage partner never graces our door. Some of us seek friends. But for reasons we don't understand, we struggle to find and keep friends. We meet people, but they abandon us, fail to return our calls, or decline our repeated invitations.

Bullied. Are we unlovable when an entire group of people treats us badly?

We continually struggle at work and are passed over for promotions. Others don't invite us to join them for lunch. Alone at our desks, we hear laughter coming from the next office and hear the hushed voices talk about us behind our backs. Finally, our workday ends as coworkers make cruel comments as we walk to our car.

Sometimes it's our families who treat us badly. We're like Cinderella. They expect us to do all of the family chores and serve our parents and siblings. We tread lightly with our words, trying to avoid an explosive conflict for which we will be blamed. The family seems to blame us for everything.

Don't believe that you're unlovable. In all cases, you are lovable. We are lovable. We're not only lovable, but each of us is also loved.

I finally faced my youthful choices and turned myself and my sins over to Jesus. Although I'd known, intellectually, for years that God forgave me for my choices, I didn't accept his forgiveness into my heart. I denied his love, his grace, and his mercy until I realized that God loves me as his child. God – the Almighty, the Creator, the One and Only – calls me his child.

Once I accepted Jesus as my personal Savior, and invited him into my life, into my heart, I began to live *in Christ* – in unity with him, who is in unity with God and the Holy Spirit. God is love. Thus, living in Christ, I live under the warm blanket of God's love. God's love surrounds me, comforts me, holds me, strengthens me, and never leaves me. God, through his Holy Spirit, in Christ Jesus, has made me his daughter.

Both loved and lovable, I live in his love. God is love. I am in him and he is in me, through Jesus.

> *For those who are led by the Spirit of God are the children of God. The Spirit you received does not make you slaves, so that you live in fear again; rather, the Spirit you received brought about your adoption to sonship. And by him we cry, "Abba, Father." The Spirit himself testifies with our spirit that we are God's children.* (Romans 8:14-16)

God calls all believers in Christ his children. It doesn't matter who we've been, or what we've done. It doesn't matter what other people have done to us in the past or what they do to us now. Why? Because as we live in Christ, God lives in us through his Spirit. God is love. His love is in us, surrounds us, carries us, holds us, supports us, blesses us, heals us, forgives us, and directs us. We live in God's love, and his love lives in us.

God is our Father. We are his sons and daughters, princes and princesses in God's kingdom. Loved, in Christ, through Christ.

I pray for you just as the apostle Paul prayed for the Ephesians: *I pray that Christ will live in your hearts by faith and that your life will be strong in love and be built on love. And I pray that you and all God's holy people will have the power to understand the greatness of Christ's love—how wide and how long and how high and how deep that love is. Christ's love is greater than anyone can ever know, but I pray that you will be able to know that love. Then you can be filled with the fullness of God* (Ephesians 3:17-19 NCV). Amen.

As believers in Christ Jesus, we live in God's love. In his love, we are children of God. We are somebody because we are filled with the fullness of God.

I Will Do What I Can, Where I Am, With I AM!

Chapter 6

Do I Love God?

Have you ever told someone that you loved them and hoped they would respond in a like manner? After you finally got up the courage to say that simple sentence, "I love you," you waited for what seemed like an eternity. The response was silence, or he changed the subject. Maybe he responded with, "Let's go rent a movie."

Wait, you think to yourself. You feel embarrassed, hurt, and a little angry. *Maybe he didn't hear me.* So you say it again, in the most inviting manner possible. "I said, 'I love you.' Maybe you didn't hear me."

He replies, "I heard you. I just didn't know what to say."

"Don't you love me?"

"I don't know. I guess I never thought about it," he concludes. He never voices the words you hoped to hear.

> *For God so loved the world that he gave his one and only Son, that whoever believes in him shall not perish but have eternal life.* (John 3:16)

God loves each of us. Because of that love, he gave his only

Son, Jesus, to die for us, save us, and give us eternal life. God *told* us that he loves us and *showed* us that he loves us. So, if God asked, "Do you love me?" what would you say?

Would you change the subject? Would you leave the room or pretend you didn't hear? Would you go rent a movie?

If God pushed further for an answer to his question, what would you say?

For those of us raised in church, taught to believe in God and to love him, we might answer God's question quickly, almost without thought, with a definitive "Yes." That's a good start. But I ask you to search your heart. Is your answer the truth? Are you sure that you haven't been merely trained to *say* that you love him?

Maybe you know the lyrics to the song, "Do You Love Me?" from the musical *Fiddler on the Roof.* In that song, Tevye asks his wife of twenty-five years if she loves him. In her first response to the question, she suggests that he must be tired or upset and he should go lie down. He asks again, and she calls him a fool. He insists on an answer, so she lists things she has done to maintain their home and then questions why he needs to speak of love.

Does a long list of things we do in our homes, or churches, mean we love God? Maybe, but maybe not.

The Bible tells us about two sisters named Mary and Martha. You may be familiar with the story. Martha invited Jesus into her home. When he arrived, Martha worked hard to be a good hostess, while Mary (who also lived there) sat at Jesus' feet and gave him her time. This frustrated Martha. She expressed her frustration to Jesus, and he said to her, *"you are worried and upset about many things, but few things are needed—or indeed only one. Mary has chosen what is better, and it will not be taken away from her."* (See Luke 10:38-42.)

Mary gave Jesus her time and attention. She sought a

relationship. Martha, although she had good intentions, was focused on the jobs that needed doing. She wasn't focused on Jesus directly, although I'm certain her thoughts never left his side.

I've been Martha. Recently, we hosted a party at our home. As hostess, I kept myself so busy that by the time I sat down to visit with our guests, it was late, and they had already begun to leave. I provided our guests with food, drink, and the opportunity to enjoy each other's company, but my priorities didn't allow me the same opportunity to visit. If my goal was to personally visit with our guests, my plans didn't work out. Yet my intentions were good, and our guests appreciated the chance to be with each other.

It's easy to forfeit time at the feet of Jesus when we spend our time and resources to accomplish church chores or serve good causes. Many people, with all the best intentions, are quick to list the numerous volunteer jobs they do for the church or in the name of Jesus. Perhaps they work as a church usher, serve on the church council, teach Sunday school, or host the coffee hour. Maybe they volunteer at the food pantry, go on mission trips, or rake yards for the elderly.

All of these things are good and laudable things to do. However, they don't constitute time spent with Jesus, at least not directly and not necessarily with the purpose of building a relationship with him. They are Martha things, albeit mostly necessary, done with good intentions, and, in many cases, done out of love for Christ.

Let's return again to the lyrics of the song, "Do You Love Me?" from the musical *Fiddler on the Roof*. Tevye continues to press his wife and insists on an answer to his question, "Do you love me?" Finally, she lists elements of her relationship with him. She fought with him, suffered with him, and shared her bed with him. She concludes that if that's not love, she doesn't know what love is.

It's the relationship that counts, first and foremost. Then, the doing counts.

> *If I speak in the tongues of men or of angels, but*
> *do not have love, I am only a resounding gong or a*
> *clanging cymbal. If I have the gift of prophecy and*
> *can fathom all mysteries and all knowledge, and*
> *if I have a faith that can move mountains, but do*
> *not have love, I am nothing. If I give all I possess*
> *to the poor and give over my body to hardship that*
> *I may boast, but do not have love, I gain nothing.*
> (1 Corinthians 13:1-3)

Spend time with God for the purpose of getting closer to him. Talk to him through prayer at any place and at any time, whether at home, at work, while driving (but keep your eyes open), or when you're with friends. To deepen your relationship with him, read the Bible, participate in a Bible study, attend worship services or a Christian retreat. Finally, sit quietly, think about him, and try to hear what he has to say to you.

We know how much God loves us. Do we truly love him? If we do, we will long for relationship time with him. We will thirst for him, for ways to learn more about him, and for his constant presence in our lives. When we experience dry spells, periods when God seems distant, we will miss him. The times when we clearly sense his presence, we'll know the joy and peace that comes from his Holy Spirit.

As we live in relationship with Jesus, we live in a relationship of love. If we live in the love of Christ, we live in God, and God lives in us.

Unity, oneness, and love was Jesus' prayer, his dying request.

All will know that Jesus was sent by God. All who believe will be saved.

> *If anyone acknowledges that Jesus is the Son of God,*
> *God lives in them and they in God. And so we know*
> *and rely on the love God has for us. God is love.*
> *Whoever lives in love lives in God, and God in them.*
> (1 John 4:15-16)

Jesus is the Son of God. As believers, we live in God, and he lives in us. We know his love, because God is love. His love is in each of us. We live in God's love, and his love lives in us. With God's love, we can make a difference. Through God's love, we are each somebody. It's what God does for us because he loves us. It is the only way, and it all starts with love.

I love God, just as God loves me. Say it out loud: I love God, just as God loves me. Think it, announce it, pray it, live it.

I Will Do What I Can, Where I Am, With I AM!

Chapter 7

Love God Out Loud

I love God. I love Jesus. Can you see my love for God? It's written all over my face. Can you see the dreamy look in my eyes when I think of him? No? I'm here on the loveseat in our house as I type these words into my laptop. Isn't my love for God clearly evident by the length of time I sit in the loveseat, the official chair of love? No? Well then, what might I do to make my love for God more evident? How do I exhibit my love for God?

When we love, it causes us to *do* things for the one we love. We love out loud.

First there is the relationship and then there is the doing.

Our daughters and I have entered a stage of relationship transition. Although they're both adults now and live on their own, I continue to want to help them. Sometimes they believe I'm over-mothering them. I disagree, of course. Both in their twenties and married, they don't need "mothering," even though I know they appreciate that I love them, and they sometimes still need some "mom" time. I understand they want to live independently and make their own decisions. However, I don't always strike the right balance.

For example, when our older daughter was looking for employment, as a heavy data person, I searched for job leads and provided her with a seemingly endless stream of e-mails with new job postings. I intended to be helpful and wanted to show her the many avenues and ideas for her employment future. I assumed she would consider the ideas, some good and some not so good, and focus her job search as she deemed appropriate.

She interpreted my help as pushy and overly motherly. She thought I expected her to pursue *all* of the job postings. Tensions rose but were ultimately dispelled when we reached a mutual understanding that I only intended to provide the data, and that decisions regarding employment were hers to make. Together, we're getting better at this transitional stage, the necessary shift from a parent-child relationship to a parent-adult relationship.

The point of that story is that I love our daughters dearly, and my love for them shines through by the things I offer to do for them and with them. Love for others exhibits itself through our actions. Love is a verb, a word of action. We show our love by what we do. When we love deeply, we love out loud.

In John 21, Jesus asked Simon Peter three times if he loved him. Each time, Peter replied in the positive: *you know that I love you.* After the first question, Jesus told Peter to *feed my lambs.* After the second question, Jesus told Peter to *take care of my sheep.* After the third question, Jesus told Peter to *feed my sheep.* After each question and affirmation of Peter's love, Jesus told Peter to do something. Specifically, Jesus told Peter to show his love by caring for and feeding those who believe in Jesus, not necessarily with food and shelter, but with the gospel message, a message of sacrifice and atonement for our sins, which Peter would soon understand. Jesus told Peter to *do* something, to love out loud.

Throughout the Bible, all believers are told to do things out of love. We are not to sit dreamily on the loveseat and float through life in our love of God. No, instead we are supposed to do things out of our love for God. If we love God, we will demonstrate love, not just feel love.

I will do. I will put actions behind my love for the one I love most. I will do love for God. My demonstration of love for God shows others how much I love him. We do love for God because he did (and still does) love us. His greatest act of love came through his Son, Jesus. *For God so loved the world that he gave his one and only Son, that whoever believes in him shall not perish but have eternal life* (John 3:16). God gave us his Son, the life of his Son, so that we would have life in him, forever. God did love by the greatest possible act. Through the sacrifice of his only Son, God loved out loud and continues to demonstrate his love in our lives today, all day, every day.

I love God. I will take action because of my love for him and I will return love for the love he has given me. Through my actions, I will show my love for God.

What are we to do? What does this active form of love look like? I find that doing love for our daughters is better received when I first find out what they want. It's a little like giving advice. Don't we all hate getting unsolicited advice? Who likes advice on how to improve upon the things we do or the ways we behave? Such advice, when unsolicited, presumes that the advisor believes we aren't doing or behaving as well as we might. Who likes to have someone insist that we do things their way? Unsolicited advice frequently sounds a lot like criticism.

Sometimes unsolicited *help* is viewed in the same manner. Our daughters occasionally view my help as criticism. Their perception is that I don't believe they're sufficiently competent to handle the situation on their own. That is not my intent. In my heart, I'm trying to help make their lives more pleasant.

To do love, in the most loving way, we must understand what the one we love wants us to do, and not just assume we know what's best.

What does this active form of love for God look like? What would God like us to do?

Jesus said, *"If you love me, keep my commands"* (John 14:15). That's what God asks of us, to keep his commands. So we demonstrate our love for God, Jesus, and the Holy Spirit when we keep God's commands. We love God through obedience.

> *And this is love: that we walk in obedience to his*
> *commands. As you have heard from the beginning,*
> *his command is that you walk in love.* (2 John 6)

To show God we love him, we *do* something. We live lives of obedience. We treasure and try to follow his commands.

In Old Testament days, God placed many commands on his people. They were very specific and covered day-to-day things. God gave instructions as to the types of animals that could be used for food, the sacrifices required to atone for one's sins, the appropriate punishment for actions or crimes against one's neighbors, who could enter the temple generally speaking, and who could enter the most sacred areas of the temple. These represent just a few of the Old Testament commands.

On top of the commands found in the Old Testament, the Pharisees (religious leaders who came into power around 150 BC) developed their own set of laws, over six hundred of them, to be followed in order to properly live out one's faith.[1] This created an impossible world in which to live, a judgmental form of religious tyranny with power held by the self-righteous Pharisees.

Jesus called the Pharisees hypocrites. He noted that the Pharisees were seated in positions of authority, but warned, *So you must be careful to do everything they tell you. But do not do what they do, for they do not practice what they preach. They tie up heavy, cumbersome loads and put them on other people's shoulders, but they themselves are not willing to lift a finger to move them. Everything they do is done for people to*

---

1   "Pharisaic Laws," *www.bible.org/illustration/pharisaic-laws* (February 2, 2009).

see (Matthew 23:3-5a). The Pharisees were self-important and liked their positions of honor, influence, and power. Failure to follow their laws carried serious and often deadly consequences.

In contrast, Jesus boiled all the biblical commands down to just two commands. Specifically, Jesus said that the most important commandment is this: *Love the Lord your God with all your heart and with all your soul and with all your mind and with all your strength* (Mark 12:30). He added, *The second is this: 'Love your neighbor as yourself.' There is no commandment greater than these* (Mark 12:31). For this, I am grateful. It's a short-enough list for me to remember.

> *Above all, clothe yourselves with love, which*
> *binds us all together in perfect harmony.*
> (Colossians 3:14 NLT)

Let's start with the first and greatest commandment: *Love the Lord your God with all your heart and with all your soul and with all your mind and with all your strength.* How do we do that? What does a person *do* to show that they love God with their entire being, their heart, their mind, their soul, and their strength?

What does it look like to love God with all of our heart? Think about the people and things you love. Does the list include your spouse, children, or grandchildren? How about your parents, siblings, or a significant other? Do you love your job or career? Are you in constant pursuit of money? Do you love your social media friends? What are your passions in life? Do you live for your hobbies, for fishing, boating, camping, or bicycling? How about woodworking or hunting?

What items do you love more than you love God? Don't answer too quickly. It's easy to give the answer that we know is the *best* answer: "God is first in my life. He is above all things." But is that answer the truth?

Do we put sports events over worship on Sunday? Would we rather sleep than go to church? Is our worship time limited to Sunday mornings? Do we limit our prayer time to set times of the day, such as at mealtime and before bed? Does our pursuit of money take priority over the time we spend with Jesus? Is what we give to God limited to what is left over after we pay the bills? Do we spend more time each week on the Internet than we do with the Lord, or play computer games more often than we pray?

While [Jesus] *was in Bethany, reclining at the table in the home of Simon the Leper, a woman came with an alabaster jar of very expensive perfume, made of pure nard. She broke the jar and poured the perfume on his head* (Mark 14:3). Judas Iscariot criticized the woman's actions. He said that the perfume could have been sold for a year's wages, and the money could have been used to help the poor. He accused her of being wasteful. But she showed her love for Jesus with that perfume.

How many of us have given up something of such financial value for God? Many people tithe from their earnings to the church. After ten years, they will have given to God what this woman sacrificed in one evening.

I also think about Abraham and his son Isaac, the son of his wife, Sarah. Abraham was one hundred years old when Sarah gave birth to Isaac. Sarah had been barren up until that time. Yet God chose to bless them with a son in their old age. As a mother, I know the depth of love I feel for our daughters. I can only imagine how the feelings of love might be amplified for someone who waited a lifetime for the blessing of a child. But even with the depth of love that Abraham likely felt for Isaac, when God tested Abraham and asked that he sacrifice Isaac as a burnt offering, Abraham obeyed. At the last minute, God stopped Abraham and provided a ram for the sacrifice.

Could I put God above our daughters' lives and respond

with obedience in such an extreme test of my faith? Do I truly love God more than our daughters? What else in my life would test the limits of my love for God if he commanded obedience? I pray that he saves me from such tests.

Do I love God? Do I love him with all my heart, soul, mind, and strength? I do love him, but what does that look like? Can others *see* my love for him?

What does it mean to love God with all one's heart, soul, mind, and strength? It means to love God with our entire being and all that we are. To do love with our entire being means that we do, prepare, organize, persuade, think, reflect, ponder, consider, meditate, contemplate, discuss, say, converse, chat, respond, answer, reply, help, aid, support, work, play, learn, study, absorb, and act in ways which honor God and show praise for God above all others, above all things. Think of a verb, any form of action or inaction. Choose to do it or not do it in such a way that you honor God. Raise him up through your life of praise and make your love for God evident in all that you do. Love God out loud!

> *Whatever you do, work at it with all your heart, as working for the Lord, not for human masters, since you know that you will receive an inheritance from the Lord as a reward. It is the Lord Christ you are serving.* (Colossians 3:23-24)

When my love for God is evident in all I do, I will make a difference. As I love God out loud, I will be somebody. As you love God out loud, with all your being, you too will be somebody.

I Will Do What I Can, Where I Am, With I AM!

Chapter 8

Love Others Out Loud

A number of years ago, I prayed the same prayer every day, many times each day. It went something like this: Dear Father God. Bless me today in such a way that when others see me, they don't really see me, but instead they see the love of Jesus. Enable me to reflect Jesus' love in all that I do and in all that I say. Amen. Come, Lord Jesus. Amen.

In time, I felt a sense of peace about me and acted with a genuine kindness toward others in all encounters. I knew this inner peace and new outward demeanor came from God and it felt amazing. However, that's not the point of this story.

People treated me differently. As one example, I decided to get a coffee while at the airport. The woman at the counter looked up at me as she handed me my coffee, her face softened, and she said there would be no charge. She said it was a gift from her to me. Others complimented me on my hair. Strangers intentionally got up from their table, walked across the restaurant to my table, and told me they loved my hair. (I still have the same haircut, but no one bothers to compliment me on it anymore.) Once, when traveling for work, I brought a book with me to the restaurant to help pass the time while I waited for my dinner. Enjoying my book, I hadn't noticed a delay in service, but the restaurant manager came to my table and explained that there would be no charge for my dinner. He believed I had waited too long for service. I assured him that I was fine and hadn't noticed a delay. Yet he insisted that I wouldn't be charged for dinner.

Those are just a few examples of the new way others treated me. I knew why. They saw something about me that drew them to me. It wasn't my personality or my physical appearance that they saw. They saw something special, something different, and that something drew them to me. What they saw was the love of Christ and the Lord's peace and love within me. They may not have recognized or understood what it was that drew them to me. It wasn't my haircut. It wasn't me at all. They saw Jesus and his love.

As I mentioned earlier, on the final night before his crucifixion, Jesus prayed that all believers would be one with each other and one with Jesus, just as he is one with God. As we live in unity with Christ, God's love will be in us. With God's love in us, we can demonstrate God's love, share it with those around us, and love them out loud. Jesus knew that through such love, all will know that God sent him to save us (John 17).

Jesus' love should be evident in all that we do. It's possible to live in such a way that all those who encounter us will see something special, something different, something that draws them to Christ. When God's love overflows, all people will know that Jesus is Lord.

As I put Jesus first, and prayed to live in him, through him, with him, and like him, others saw him. I was the evidence that Jesus is Lord, and others saw him. During that time in my life, God's love filled me and shone all around me. I shared his love in the simplest of ways because his love overflowed. I loved out loud in the simplest of encounters with others. Some people recognized Jesus' love, and others thought it was my haircut. But they each saw something they knew was good. (And we all know the haircut wasn't that special.) In time, the Holy Spirit will enable them to understand and know the truth.

> *Dear friends, let us love one another, for love comes*
> *from God. Everyone who loves has been born of*
> *God and knows God. Whoever does not love does*
> *not know God, because God is love. This is how*
> *God showed his love among us: He sent his one and*
> *only Son into the world that we might live through*
> *him. This is love: not that we loved God, but that*
> *he loved us and sent his Son as an atoning sacrifice*
> *for our sins. Dear friends, since God so loved us, we*
> *also ought to love one another. No one has ever seen*
> *God; but if we love one another, God lives in us and*
> *his love is made complete in us.*
>
> *This is how we know that we live in him and he in*
> *us: He has given us of his Spirit. And we have seen*
> *and testify that the Father has sent his Son to be the*
> *Savior of the world. If anyone acknowledges that*
> *Jesus is the Son of God, God lives in them and they*
> *in God. And so we know and rely on the love God*
> *has for us.*
>
> *God is love. Whoever lives in love lives in God, and*
> *God in them.* (1 John 4:7-16)

As we live in God's love, showered with his love and covered in his love, we have his love to spare and share. The apostle John wrote the verses quoted above. As one of the original twelve disciples, he lived with Jesus, traveled with Jesus, learned from Jesus, and listened to Jesus' public and private teachings. He wrote the gospel of John and three letters known as 1 John, 2 John, and 3 John. Finally, he penned the book of Revelation.

John knew Jesus' love personally and directly. He experienced love from the Son of God himself, in person, as Jesus lived on earth as a man. John lived in close proximity to Jesus and walked daily in his love. As a result of that firsthand experience, John teaches that we should live as Jesus lived. In 2 John 6, he tells us that Jesus commands us to walk in love. In the Amplified Bible, Classic Edition, the words *walk in love* are described further to mean *guided by it and following it.*

In other words, Jesus asks each of us to live out his love, guided by the way he lived and treated others. John reminds us to follow Jesus' actions and implement them in our daily lives in the way we treat others.

> *Imitate God, therefore, in everything you do,*
> *because you are his dear children. Live a life filled*
> *with love, following the example of Christ. He loved*
> *us and offered himself as a sacrifice for us, a pleas-*
> *ing aroma to God.* (Ephesians 5:1-2 NLT)

Imitate God, therefore, in everything you do, the apostle Paul says in his letter to the Ephesians. Imitate God because you are his children.

Children imitate others, particularly those they love, those who receive positive attention for their actions, or those who they believe are having fun. It can be good to imitate others' behavior, particularly in families where good parents lead by example. Good parents teach their children how to live when they model what they teach. They say, "Do as I do." And that's what God says through the apostle Paul: "Do as I do."

Whoever claims to live in him must live as Jesus did.
(1 John 2:6)

Jesus' actions and words exuded love for others, even up to

the point of death on the cross. The ways Jesus showed his love to others are many.

Here's only a short list of the ways Jesus showed his love to others:

- Celebrated joyous occasions (John 2:1-11)
- Helped his friends save face (John 2:1-11)
- Shared in the sorrows of his friends (John 11:34-36)
- Changed the lives of sinners (Matthew 9:9-13; Mark 2:15-17; Luke 5:29-32; John 4:1-26)
- Forgave sins (Matthew 9:1-2; Mark 2:5; Luke 5:20; 7:36-50)
- Protected the accused from injustice (John 8:2-11)
- Listened (Mark 5:32-33; Luke 8:47-48)
- Healed the sick (Matthew 14:34-36; 15:29-31; Mark 5:32-33; 6:53-56; Luke 4:38-40; 5:12-13)
- Fed the hungry (Mark 6:30-44; 8:1-10; Luke 9:12-17)
- Renewed sight to the blind (Matthew 20:29-34; Mark 8:22-26; John 9:1-12)
- Forgave his enemies (Luke 23:34)
- Lovingly changed sinful behaviors (Luke 19:1-10; John 4:1-39; 8:11)
- Taught truth to the crowds (Matthew 5, 6, 7, 13; Mark 6:34; Luke 6:17-49)
- Loved children (Mark 10:14)
- Calmed stormy waters (Matthew 8:23-26; Mark 4:35-40)
- Served others with humility (John 13:1-5)
- Provided for his mother upon his death (John 19:26-27)
- Prayed for all (John 17:20-21)
- Gave his life for all people (Matthew 27; Mark 15; Luke 23; John 19)

To summarize, Jesus acted with compassion and loved all, even his enemies (Matthew 14:14; 15:32; Mark 6:34). In the same way, we are called to love others. With the same mind-set as Christ, we are to act with humility and serve others (Philippians 2:5-8).

> *Therefore, as God's chosen people, holy and dearly loved, clothe yourselves with compassion, kindness, humility, gentleness and patience. Bear with each other and forgive one another if any of you has a grievance against someone. Forgive as the Lord forgave you. And over all these virtues put on love, which binds them all together in perfect unity.* (Colossians 3:12-14)

How do we share God's love? How do we live out God's love? Pray for Jesus to be first in your life. Remember Jesus and the example he set for us. Live with compassion and love others by your actions. Notice the need and act upon it. When we demonstrate God's love with compassion, we can improve the lives of others. We have the opportunity to help others and lovingly guide them to live lives that honor God. Through our obedience we enable others to see the heart of Jesus. We can make a difference.

I encourage you to do what you can with I AM, sharing his great love with all those around you. I will do what I can, where I am, with I AM and his love.

I Will Do What I Can, Where I Am, With I AM!

Chapter 9

Love Like Christ

Do you want to love others as Jesus loved others? Can we really do what Jesus did? I want to imitate Christ through my life and through my actions, but I'm not Jesus. How do we love others like he loved?

Jesus did miracles. The Bible provides many accounts of Jesus' miracles, healings, casting out demons, taming the storms, and even instances of bringing people back from the dead. These are amazing stories. If you read the gospel of Mark, you'll find many of these accounts described at a rapid-fire pace, because Mark's gospel is action focused and filled with the works of Jesus.

It's easy to let these miracles capture our thoughts, because they're quite amazing. Jesus gifted some of his disciples with the ability to perform similar miracles. Even today, the Holy Spirit blesses some people with the gift of healing and enables them to perform miracles in people's lives that medical doctors haven't been able to explain.

How do we imitate Jesus and share God's love? What do we do if the Holy Spirit hasn't blessed us with the gift of healing? What can we do if we are unable to stop the storm? Are we called to perform miracles? Maybe. Maybe not. It depends on what God calls each of us to do at any given time.

Whatever God calls us to do, he will enable us to do it through the gifts that are given to us by the Holy Spirit. Some of us may not yet recognize the gifts that have been given to us by the Holy Spirit, yet we're called to do what we can with I AM. When we answer God's call, we will discover that we can do amazing things.

> *Very truly I tell you, whoever believes in me will do the works I have been doing, and they will do even greater things than these, because I am going to the Father. And I will do whatever you ask in my name, so that the Father may be glorified in the Son. You may ask me for anything in my name, and I will do it.* (John 14:12-14)

So how do we answer God's call? How do we love like Jesus if we can't feed thousands with just a small amount of food? What if we are unable to drive out demons or raise people from the dead? Is it really possible to live as Jesus lived and imitate him? Absolutely! We can start by living and loving others as Jesus did. The point isn't to perform the many miracles that Jesus did for others, but rather to respond to others with the heart of Jesus, with his love.

For example, when a man with leprosy begged Jesus to heal him, the Bible tells us that Jesus understood the unfairness of this man's situation. Out of compassion and sympathy, Jesus responded. He healed him because he cared about the man, not to show off or prove that he was God's son (Mark 1:41).

Jesus healed because he cared about the man.

Then there was the time Jesus' disciples had just returned from an extended ministry trip. They attempted to find a secluded place where they could rest and talk about the past days. But the people in the area recognized Jesus and his disciples and ran to them. Again, Jesus felt compassion for the people, because *they were like sheep without a shepherd* (Mark 6:34). So instead of leaving for a quiet place, he stayed to teach them.

Jesus taught, because he cared about their spiritual condition.

One day, as Jesus taught thousands, he recognized that the people needed food. He felt sorry for them and didn't want to send them away hungry, because they might not be able to make the trip. So with just seven loaves of bread and a few fish, he fed thousands. Then he sent them on their way (Mark 8:1-10).

Jesus fed them, because he cared about their daily needs.

When the Pharisees brought a woman to Jesus who had been caught in the act of adultery, they questioned Jesus about the law of Moses and asked him if he believed she should be stoned to death. Jesus knew the Pharisees intended to trap him. He didn't disregard the law, but suggested that the first stone should be thrown by one who had never sinned. Then he looked down and wrote something in the dirt with his finger. When the woman's accusers heard this, they all left (John 8:1-11).

Jesus saved this woman from a horrible death, forgave her, and told her to sin no more. He offered compassionate justice.

Mary and Martha's brother, Lazarus, became very ill. Jesus loved Lazarus, but when he received word of his illness and a request for help, he delayed his trip until Lazarus was already dead. Jesus knew he intended to bring Lazarus back to life. But when he saw Mary crying, Jesus wept. He wept out of sympathy for Mary's grief and the grief of the other mourners (John 11:1-35).

Jesus wept, because he cared about Mary. He felt her broken heart.

Finally, in the end, Jesus gave his life for us out of love. While he was still alive, Jesus told his disciples that he came to serve, minister to others, and save the lives of many through his own death (Mark 10:45).

Jesus loved so deeply that he, of his own will, died to save our lives.

Jesus loved others and showed it not only in words and through his teachings, but also by the way he lived. He cared about all people's physical, emotional, and spiritual well-being. Through his love, he healed them, provided for them, taught them, encouraged them, forgave them, and led them to a better path in life.

We don't need to perform miracles to imitate Jesus and live out God's love in our lives. We live out God's love when we care about the physical, emotional, and spiritual well-being of others. Through our actions, we show them love. We can comfort them in their troubles, provide for them when they are unable to provide for themselves, teach them, encourage them, forgive them, and lead them to a better path in life.

In his letter to the Romans, the apostle Paul describes what love looks like when we demonstrate God's love in our relationships with others. He instructs us to hate evil and stick with what is good. We must act out of devotion to others and show them honor as we humble ourselves. We maintain our love for God as we serve him at all times. The apostle Paul goes on to urge us to *be joyful in hope, patient in affliction, faithful in prayer,* and to share with those in need. When we're instructed to love, this includes our enemies. We are to celebrate with others as they celebrate, and mourn with them as they mourn. And as far as it depends on us, we must try to live harmoniously with others, in peace, and avoid pride. Finally, revenge is not ours to seek; it is to be left in God's just hands (Romans 12:9-19).

Love requires our action. It means that we will *do* something.

*Dear children, let us not love with words or speech
but with actions and in truth.* (1 John 3:18)

Live in Christ and in God's love. Live out God's love and
love others out loud. Our opportunity to reach the world starts
today in our homes, families, neighborhoods, and communities, to change hearts for Christ. We can change the world and
reach the lost through Christ, when we live in unity with him
and live out God's love in all that we do. This was Jesus' dying
prayer. God will certainly answer Jesus' prayer, and he calls us
to be part of that answer.

> *As a prisoner for the Lord, then, I urge you to live
> a life worthy of the calling you have received. Be
> completely humble and gentle; be patient, bearing
> with one another in love. Make every effort to keep
> the unity of the Spirit through the bond of peace.*
> (Ephesians 4:1-3)

We are called to be somebody by loving others out loud. How
do you choose to respond? Are you willing to say, "Yes, Lord,
I will"? Will you do what you can with I AM? If we respond
with "I will," as we share the love of Jesus and live out God's
love, we will lead the world to Jesus. They will know that Jesus
is God's Son, the Messiah.

I will do what I can, where I am, with I AM by sharing God's
love for others through my actions.

I Will Do What I Can, Where I Am, With I AM!

Chapter 10

Love Out Loud through Action

W hat does it look like to love others out loud? What does it look like to imitate the heart of Jesus?

Like everyone, when I left high school, I needed to select a career path, an educational and work-life direction. My high school classes had been easy for me. I knew my future path would involve college, but my field of choice evaded my imagination. My childhood dream didn't involve a profession. Instead, I wanted to be wealthy and have a very comfortable life. So my work-life direction and my education had to open doors to jobs that provided the potential for significant income.

My vision focused on me. It was all about using my education, skills, talents, and abilities to take care of me. In fact, I believed, without question, that God blessed me with all of my abilities to make my life better. I had ambition, a selfish ambition.

Do nothing out of selfish ambition or vain conceit.
Rather, in humility value others above yourselves,
not looking to your own interests but each of you to
the interests of the others. (Philippians 2:3-4)

In those early years, it never crossed my mind that God might have given me my skills, talents, gifts, and abilities to serve others. The apostle Peter said that the gifts given to us by God *are* to be used to serve others. When we love God with all of our heart, soul, mind, and strength, we show that love when we love others, help others, share with others, care for others, and act with the heart of Jesus (1 Peter 4:10).

Through helpful action, service to others, people will see and know God.

Nowhere does Jesus command that we should strive to serve ourselves, work for wealth, and become better than those around us. Instead, he tells us that the second greatest commandment is to love others. After God, it's all about others, about loving others, even those we don't like. Jesus explained that it's not enough to love those who love us (Luke 6:32). Instead, we are to love those we find difficult to love, those who aren't particularly likeable, and those who don't like us – our enemies. This type of love is neither a suggestion nor simply a nice gesture. It's a command. Jesus said, *My command is this: Love each other as I have loved you* (John 15:12).

> *Therefore, as God's chosen people, holy and dearly loved, clothe yourselves with compassion, kindness, humility, gentleness and patience. Bear with each other and forgive one another if any of you has a grievance against someone. Forgive as the Lord forgave you. And over all these virtues put on love, which binds them all together in perfect unity.* (Colossians 3:12-14)

The Bible is full of stories of love, accounts of people doing good and loving acts for others, friends, enemies, family, and even strangers. Through these glimpses into history, we see what it looks like to love others with the heart of Jesus.

We find an example in the story about Rebekah. Abraham wanted his son Isaac to marry a woman from his own family line. So he asked his head servant to travel back to his homeland to find a suitable wife for his son. As he arrived in town, the servant prayed and asked God to reveal the right woman for Isaac. He asked for a sign. The right woman would not only grant his request for a drink of water but also offer to draw water for his ten camels. When Rebekah arrived at the well, the servant asked for a drink of water. Rebekah gave him a drink and then drew water for his camels. This was no small act of kindness. One thirsty camel is able to drink thirty gallons of water!

Rebekah showed her love for others when she had compassion and helped a total stranger with the hard work of her hands. She drew perhaps as many as three hundred gallons of water from the well.

Help those in need, including strangers.

Another example is the love and friendship between David and King Saul's son Jonathan. The Bible tells us that Jonathan loved David with his life. He gave David his sword and his armor. This enabled David to be a successful warrior for King Saul. As David's success grew, his popularity with the people of Saul's kingdom also grew. The attention David received made King Saul very jealous, so jealous that he wanted to kill David (1 Samuel 18:1-12). When Jonathan learned of his father's plans, he stuck up for David and tried to settle King Saul's heart (1 Samuel 19:1-7). In time, however, King Saul again wanted David dead. Although Jonathan didn't initially believe that his father intended to kill David, he worked out a creative plan to discern his father's intent, communicate that intent to David from a distance, and save David's life by helping him flee. Jonathan did all this even though he knew that he might have to face the anger of his father (1 Samuel 20).

Jonathan loved his friend David. He first showed that love

for his friend when he helped him succeed. Later, Jonathan looked beyond his own personal risk of angering his father. He used his mind and craftiness to enable David to escape safely.

Help others to succeed and protect them, even if you put your own safety or comfort at risk.

We serve others when we forgive them for the things they've done to us. By doing so, we help free them from their bondage of guilt. Jesus said, *"But to you who are listening I say: Love your enemies, do good to those who hate you, bless those who curse you, pray for those who mistreat you"* (Luke 6:27-28).

Jesus didn't just *say* we should love our enemies. He *showed* love for his enemies even in the most extreme circumstances. While on the cross and as he faced death, after being betrayed, wrongly sentenced to death, humiliated, beaten, whipped with forty lashes, mocked, and nailed to the cross to die, Jesus prayed for his enemies. He said, *"Father, forgive them, for they do not know what they are doing"* (Luke 23:34).

At one point in my career, I worked with someone who did many things to ruin my employment opportunities for her own personal gain. The employment-related attacks went on for years, even though I accepted a position in another department to avoid them. I eventually left the company. I was hurt and angry. I wanted revenge, but I simply resorted to prayer. I tried to give my hurt and anger to God, and asked him to release me from my anger and to someday open her eyes, so she would realize what she had done to me. God granted my request and opened her eyes. About ten years after I left that employment situation, we saw each other at a conference. She tearfully apologized for how badly she had treated me.

Upon hearing her words, my mind raced. *What should I say? Do I say that I forgive her? Do I tell her not to worry about it? Do I tell her it's all okay?*

I stammered a bit and basically said nothing. She hurriedly

walked away. I didn't serve her by forgiving her. I should have responded like Joseph, the young man with the coat of many colors. When his brothers went to Egypt to seek food during the days of famine, Joseph exhibited love toward them. He forgave them for selling him as a slave and said to them, *"I am your brother Joseph, the one you sold into Egypt! And now, do not be distressed and do not be angry with yourselves for selling me here, because it was to save lives that God sent me ahead of you"* (Genesis 45:4b-5).

Joseph understood that God allowed his brothers to sell him into slavery so he could serve his family and others according to God's plan for his life. Like Joseph, God also had a plan for me. He moved me out of that employment situation so I could serve others according to God's call on my life. I knew that to be true when my previous co-worker apologized to me. Yet I didn't respond as Joseph did toward his brothers. I missed a critical moment, a significant opportunity to love someone I once viewed as an enemy.

> *"You have heard that it was said, 'Love your neighbor and hate your enemy.' But I tell you, love your enemies and pray for those who persecute you, that you may be children of your Father in heaven."*
> (Matthew 5:43-45a)

Forgive others and pray for those who persecute you.

Then there's the story of Ruth and how she showed love to her mother-in-law, Naomi. Naomi and her husband were from Bethlehem. They had two sons, and each was married to a Moabite woman. To the great misfortune of the women, all three men died. When Naomi decided to return to Bethlehem, she urged her daughters-in-law to return to their homes, to their families, where each woman would likely be supported again by her parents and perhaps even find another husband. After much protest and many tears, one daughter-in-law returned home. But Ruth refused. She pledged her love and loyalty to Naomi and remained by her side (Ruth 1).

Ruth gave up a plan for personal security and a future husband to remain faithful to her mother-in-law. She looked beyond herself and loved Naomi with her soul, a soul set on loyalty.

Be loyal.

Esther also went to great lengths to help her family and, ultimately, all Israelites. Through an unusual turn of events, King Xerxes brought a young Jewish girl named Esther into his harem. Esther kept her Jewish heritage a secret as she was trained to properly behave and serve the king. She won his favor and eventually became his queen. Sometime later, one of the king's men plotted to destroy all the Jews who lived in the kingdom. Esther's uncle, who had raised Esther like a father after her parents died, told her about the plot to kill the Jews. He pleaded with her to take action.

In those days, no one was allowed to simply enter the presence of the king. They had to be invited or risk being beheaded. This law even applied to the queen. Esther explained to her uncle that if she went to King Xerxes it would be very dangerous, because he had not called for her in quite some time. However, after prayer and fasting, Esther went to the king. Her brave actions foiled the plot against the Jews and saved them all. (See the book of Esther.) Esther looked beyond herself and even risked her life to act out of love for her people.

God calls us to do what's right for the greater good. He calls us to look beyond our personal interests. He calls us to do this even when a decision for the greater good creates risk. We must be willing to accept risk to our reputations, relationships, health, finances, employment, or safety when the greater good is at stake.

I will do what I can. I will love others as myself.

Some of us have chosen jobs or volunteer in ways that clearly serve others. A partial list includes the following:

- Nurse
- Doctor
- Firefighter
- First responder
- Nursing home attendant
- Daycare worker
- Teacher
- Soccer coach
- Pastor
- Church leader

A complete list of possibilities would be extensive. When our work is our passion and we truly care about the people we serve, we show love for others.

Whether we serve others through our employment or in volunteer situations, when we make the lives of others better, we show our love for God. Jesus made this abundantly clear when he described to his disciples how people would be divided into two groups, the sheep and the goats. He will put some people to the right and others to the left. Then he will say to those on the right, *'Come, you who are blessed by my Father; take your inheritance, the kingdom prepared for you since the creation of the world. For I was hungry and you gave me something to eat, I was thirsty and you gave me something to drink, I was a stranger and you invited me in, I needed clothes and you clothed me, I was sick and you looked after me, I was in prison and you came to visit me'* (Matthew 25:34-36). The people asked Jesus when they did such things for him. Jesus replied, *'Truly I tell you, whatever you did for one of the least of these brothers and sisters of mine, you did for me'* (Matthew 25:40).

We are called to help those in need, particularly those who struggle to help themselves, whether they're hungry, sick, poor, or in prison.

Loving others with action doesn't need to be complicated. It can be evident in the way we treat others throughout the day. Do you listen to your children when they try to get your attention? Do you treat the waiter or waitress at the restaurant respectfully? Do you look beyond yourself so that you notice the potential needs of those around you? If you notice a particular need, do you step in and help? Are your motives pure, or do you look for something in return?

I'll never forget when we purchased our current home. We didn't move in until our other home sold. It was November, and we needed someone to plow the driveway during the winter if it snowed. I didn't know anyone in the area with a plowing service and hadn't met the neighbors yet. But I knew one neighbor's name. So I called him.

After I explained what I needed, my neighbor readily said, "Sure, I can do that."

"Wonderful! Thank you so much!" I replied. "How do you want me to pay you – after each time, monthly, or at the end of the season?"

My neighbor quickly retorted, "I don't want to get paid. I said I'd do it. I'll do it for nothing. That's what neighbors do for each other."

That's what neighbors do. Love your neighbor.

Like my neighbor, I can be kind and helpful to those around me. I can greet others with a smile and treat them respectfully, particularly when they help or serve me. I can listen intentionally, trying to hear what they say, to discern whether their words or body language indicate a cry for help.

In our self-centered society, it's often difficult to notice the needs of others and offer to help. It's easy to forget that we're not the center of the universe. Think of the many times you've hurried past all of the houses on your street, focused on your ultimate destination. When you did that, did you notice the mother in her front yard playing with her children who wished you would slow down?

It's also common to conclude that we're too busy to help others. I frequently have good intentions with no follow-through. I'm too busy; I've overbooked my schedule. I wonder how those excuses will fly when God asks me what I did for others during my earthly life. Maybe it's time to reprioritize some aspects of my life.

In our overly booked lifestyles, we're often short on time. Some of our jobs require long hours. Some of us work a second job to support the needs of our families. Our kids' activities eat up our time in many good but exhausting ways. Many neighborhoods aren't safe enough to allow our children to play in the park without supervision. As our parents age, they require help on a regular basis. The immediate needs of our families can be overwhelming. It may seem impossible to love our neighbors through action.

God will enable you with the time and ability when he calls you to action. Since we know that, will you notice the need and do what you can? Will you love others with your actions? Will you commit to it?

I will look beyond myself so that I recognize the needs around me and respond to those needs out of love. I will do what I can where I am, loving those around me with action.

I Will Do What I Can, Where I Am, With I AM!

Chapter 11

I Can Where I Am

Imagine you're in a quiet office, a secret-agent sort of place. You just received an urgent delivery. In the package is an audio message, one you can listen to on your new electronic device. You know the message will define your next mission. As you prepare to listen to the message, you become nervous, anxious, and excited. The message is from "The Boss." He says, "Your mission, should you choose to accept it, will be to love me with all your heart, with all your soul, with all your mind, and with all your strength. As always, you have carte blanche as to the methods and lifestyle you choose in order to accomplish this mission. As usual, this electronic device and its message will self-destruct within one minute."

Mission Impossible. Are you old enough to remember the television show, which aired from 1966 to 1973? I only vaguely remember the show. At the beginning of each show the secret agent received from "the Secretary" (the agent's boss) a new message recorded on an audio tape. It described the mission, which served as the plot for the show that day. The missions always presented elements of complexity and danger.

God has a plan, or mission, for each of us. I assume most of us have not received an audio recording which defines the details of our mission. But we have his Word. Jesus tells us that the Great Commandment requires us to love the Lord our God with all of our heart, soul, mind, and strength. We are to love God with all of our passions, abilities, thoughts, character, and influence. Our mission is to love him with our entire being.

In *Mission Impossible*, the secret agent had the option to accept or decline the mission. God offers us the option to accept or decline our mission from him. We can choose to accept the mission to love God with our entire being, or we can choose to take another path.

In *Mission Impossible*, the secret agent possessed complete freedom to pursue the mission using any method he deemed appropriate. Similarly, we have the freedom to choose how we pursue our mission within our own life circumstances. Questions concerning who, with whom, how, where, and when are all choices that are left up to us to decide. Compare it to your career choice. Did you choose to go to college, technical school, or begin to work right out of high school? Once you completed school, did you choose to work for a company or start your own business? Or did you choose to be a homemaker, wife, and mother? Did you ever wonder if you chose the right path?

If we choose to accept God's mission, we accept the responsibility to exhibit our love for him in all of our thoughts, in all that we do, and through all of our relationships, both in our personal lives and in our work lives. Based on this one commandment, the Great Commandment, we all have the same mission. But we are assigned to pursue the mission within our individual circumstances.

I will do what I can where I am.

God placed us in families, jobs, churches, communities,

states, and countries, at this particular time in history, so that as we live out our mission in life, his purposes are fulfilled.

God created us to do good works which he prepared in advance for us to do (Ephesians 2:10). He has offered each of us a personal mission. Just as in *Mission Impossible*, some of our missions will be challenging, exciting, and even life threatening. For others, the mission will require a deep commitment of care and compassion for others. For some, their mission may seem mundane, at least for a time, while another's mission appears thrilling. Whatever the specifics, I'm certain that all missions from God will be extraordinarily rewarding. All missions will provide the opportunity to reflect him and to act as his hands, feet, and heart in honor of him.

Somebody needs to accept the mission.

Do you accept his mission for your life? Will you do what you can where you are today, physically, relationally, emotionally, spiritually, and financially? Will you say yes to God and accept his mission for your life today? Will you commit to it?

I will love God out loud when I love others where I am physically, relationally, emotionally, spiritually, and financially. As I do what I can where I am, I will be somebody.

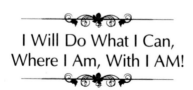

I Will Do What I Can, Where I Am, With I AM!

Chapter 12

I Can Where I Am – Physically

Our daughter Chelsy wrote the following shortly after she left for Guatemala to live for an unknown period of time.[2]

"I guess the real question is, what is the dream?

"Anybody who knows me knows this is a continually evolving question and maybe there is not an end or a final goal to my dream. It's one that will be ongoing until the day I die.

"I guess at the root of all dreams is the desire to be happy. If you really think about what dreams you've had, they likely all come down to being happy. Feel free to agree or disagree, but that is what I have observed in both my life and the lives of others. No one wakes up and dreams of doing things that will make them sad or upset. The biggest difference between each other's dreams, then, would be what makes a person happy. That dream of happiness may come from money, success in a profession, fame, a family, pleasing those around you, and so much more. But is that it? Can we truly be happy with these things? Are those things all we have to live for?

---

2   Used with permission.

"Psalm 37:4 says, *Take delight in the* LORD, *and he will give you the desires of your heart.*

"The desires of my heart? I'm not sure I know what I truly desire. Fortunately, God knows me better than I know myself.

"What if we changed the focus of our dreams to others and what will make them happy? What if our dreams matched God's plan for us? I can't say my dream matches God's plan all the time. I definitely tend to look out for me before others more often than I would like. I frequently believe I know what is best for me, despite how far off I may really be. Yet I believe there is more out there than shallow happiness. What if your dream, what if my dream, can be something that reaches beyond ourselves? What if we can seek God's dream for our lives? Maybe we could accomplish things bigger than our biggest dreams.

"Like I mentioned before, I have continually changing dreams. They pretty much revolve around the same themes, but they are changing. Common themes have been doing things I find fun, traveling, meeting new people, getting to know God, and finding that perfect job – whatever that may be. So the question after college has been, what exactly am I trying to find? What am I chasing?

"I've been praying for a long time that God would lead me to where he wants me to be. That he would guide me as to what to do and where to go. I told him I would follow willingly, if only I understood. Clearly, I cannot make my own decisions, so I am finally breaking down and giving in to my stubborn will to really seek out God's dreams for my life. So now I'm in Guatemala. If you don't know how I got here, I'll give a quick summary.

"I had been living in Appleton, Wisconsin, and was not feeling like it was where I needed to be. I felt a heavy weight on my shoulders and was desperate to find a way to lift it.

God responded. He brought me this opportunity to move to Guatemala. I don't know where this fits into his plans, but I trust him. Every barrier that got in my way, I lifted up to him in prayer, and he removed it the following day, which made it more and more clear that this is where he wanted me to go. He was with me the whole time leading up to the day I left, and I know he is with me still.

"I guess I don't know what it is that I'm chasing. Yet I know I don't have to worry. Matthew 6:34 states, *Therefore do not worry about tomorrow, for tomorrow will worry about itself.*

"The dream I'm chasing is unknown to me, but I am following faithfully. Jesus said, *Therefore go and make disciples of all nations, baptizing them in the name of the Father and of the Son and of the Holy Spirit, and teaching them to obey everything I have commanded you* (Matthew 28:19-20a). We must first go. So here I am ... chasing the dream."

Chasing a dream? Was it God's dream or her dream?

Our daughter didn't understand why she was drawn to go to Guatemala, but she strongly believed that God called her to go there. So she packed a suitcase and bought a one-way airline ticket. After five months, she came home for a couple months. Then she returned to Guatemala again with another one-way airline ticket.

God calls us to do what we can where we are. Sometimes he calls us to do what we can where we are not. That's when he encourages us to move.

Do you recall the story of Abraham? God told him to pack up his family, his entire household, and move, but he didn't tell him where to go until Abraham obeyed and got on the road. Abraham was seventy-five years old at the time. He was at a point in his life where it would have been easier to kick back and relax in his reclining rocker than begin a cross-country trek with his entire household. But the Lord promised to bless him, and Abraham did what he could, by responding positively to God's call. He moved (Genesis 12:1-3; Hebrews 11:8).

How about the story of Joseph, the guy with the coat of many colors. He didn't intend to move, but his jealous brothers sold him into slavery. As a slave, and later a prisoner, through a series of unfortunate events, God moved Joseph to Egypt. There, as you'll recall, Joseph did what he could. He worked hard, learned management skills, and remained trustworthy. Ultimately, Joseph saved his entire family from certain death caused by a seven-year famine (Genesis 37, 39-47).

I encourage you to remember the story of Esther, a young Jewish girl. She lived with her uncle in a Jewish home, practiced all the usual religious and family traditions, and likely dreamed of her future as a wife and mother. With limited warning, if any at all, she found herself in the king's palace as part of his harem. God had a plan for her. While in the harem, she did what she could. She learned the ways of the king and prepared for a year to be a woman of the king's liking. Ultimately, he made her his queen. She found herself in a position of influence in accordance with God's plan.

Rahab didn't move at all. Her home was built within the outer walls of Jericho. When two spies, under the direction of Joshua, went to Jericho, they stopped at Rahab's home. She knew the spies would be killed if they were discovered at her home, so she hid them and helped them escape to safety (Joshua 1). God had a plan for Rahab, and she did what she could in her very own home.

Even Jesus did what he could where he was. Do you recall the story about the wedding at Cana? When the hosts ran out of wine, Jesus' mother said to Jesus, "They have no wine." Jesus responded that it was not yet his time. Nonetheless, he directed the servants to fill six large water jars with water and take them to the chief steward. The water became wine, the bridegroom and his family saved face with their guests, and the finest wine was served last (John 2:1-12). Jesus did what he could at the wedding. He saw a need that would have caused embarrassment to the bridegroom and his family, and he responded to that need.

These stories contain a consistent thread. Each person did what they could. They did what they knew was right in God's eyes, in the place where they were. Some left their homes. Others stayed right in their homes. Some responded with lifelong commitments, and others responded with a special act at a single point in time. However, each person responded by doing what they could where they were physically.

Are you married with two children? Do you live in suburbia and drive a mini van? Are you a powerful executive who manages a multi-billion-dollar company who commutes across the world in your personal jet? Maybe you're an unemployed or underemployed former middle manager searching for a new job and attempting to increase your network through professional conferences and seminars.

Whether at home, in the car, traveling across the country, or participating in formal and informal organizations and meetings, God calls us to do what we can for him, to dwell in his love and express it to those around us. Sometimes he calls us to act right within our own homes. Other times he calls us to move to a new location, to live, work, and interact in a new environment.

I can hear some of your thoughts. *I'm doing what I can. For example, I teach Sunday school at our church and go on a mission trip through the church every other year. It's very rewarding. I'm doing what I can at my church.* Absolutely, you're doing what you can at your church. Perhaps you fill the role of a church elder, usher, coffee server, or nursery helper. Yes, again, you are doing what you can.

However, your church life and location is, for most of us,

only a small part of your life. I challenge you to think about the rest of the week. Where are you then? Do you care for your children at home? Are you shopping, having coffee or lunch with friends, or running on the treadmill at the gym? Do you spend your time at an office, conducting sales calls, or working in retail? Where are you when you're not at your church or when you're not participating in church-related programs? Can you say that you're living out God's love in each of these places and circumstances?

Regardless of our location and physical environment, God expects us to do what we can, to live out his love for others and always do our best. He expects our best in our homes, communities, places of employment, churches, state, country, and sometimes even in another country. We are to be alert to others in need. And we are to respond to needs by helping others and sharing God's love with them.

No matter where we are, how we got there, or how long we expect to be there, we are called to do what we can as we express God's love in our service to others.

Will you commit to it?

I will. I will do what I can, where I am, physically.

I Will Do What I Can, Where I Am, With I AM!

Chapter 13

I Can Where I Am – Relationally

With those around me – family, neighbors, friends, or strangers – I will do what I can.

I was painfully shy as a child and didn't want to be teased, laughed at, or belittled. I didn't want to be noticed at all. When we had company, I hid behind the overstuffed chair in the living room, because I didn't want anyone to see me. I didn't want anyone or anything to draw attention to me. I didn't speak unless spoken to. And even then, forming a reply was extremely hard.

We lived in the same home I now live in as an adult. Our home is on a very quiet country road. One day, my husband and I sat on the front porch for over three hours as we enjoyed coffee and conversation. The traffic on our quiet road consisted of one truck, a tractor, and a bicycle. In the distance, a train whistle interfered with the country silence.

As a child, I greatly appreciated the privacy on our quiet country road. I liked the freedom that came from having no people pollution: no noise, no company, no traffic, and no one to interrupt my day.

Being an introvert often interfered with my ability to make friends.

When I was in third grade, a new girl moved to the area. On the first day of school, I noticed her right away on the bus. She was the only other girl my age on the whole bus. I was so excited and hoped she would invite me to sit in the seat with her. I gave her my best smile and hoped she would smile back. But she just stared at me. There was no twinkle in her eye, no reciprocal smile, and no invitation to join her.

I tried again the next day. As I got on the bus and walked past her seat, I smiled. I smiled the nicest smile at her. I paused by her seat, expecting her to smile in return.

Nothing. Nada. No response. No smile. No invitation to join her.

I felt rather hurt and somewhat insulted. That evening, when I got home, I went straight to the bathroom to talk to myself in the mirror. *Why doesn't she smile back?* I asked myself. *I smiled just like this*, I thought, as I looked in the mirror at what I believed would be the friendliest smile one would ever see. *Huh? That's not a smile. It feels like a smile in my face muscles, but it looks like I'm just staring.*

So I practiced a good, friendly, big smile as I looked in the mirror. I tried to remember what my muscles felt like when I saw a smile I liked. It wasn't that I didn't know how to smile. I was so timid and shy that even though I thought I was smiling, all that showed outwardly was a blank stare. No wonder I got a blank stare in return!

For much of my adult life, I struggled with meeting new people and never knew what to say. Small talk at parties was excruciatingly difficult, particularly with new people. I couldn't wait to bolt out of the conversation and find a more familiar face, unless the person was a natural chatterbox. Then I only needed to listen. As a result, I found it easier to stand apart from the others and remain quiet. I allowed others to carry the conversation and drifted toward only those with whom I felt most comfortable.

My behaviors, based on my social comfort zone, created a different impression on others than I had hoped. Some people thought I was shy. Some thought I was aloof or independent. And others thought I was simply very quiet. The truth? I was afraid I'd say something wrong or embarrassing, or that others would learn something about me that they'd find unacceptable. So it was safer to simply not talk.

My sister, on the other hand, always was and continues to be a social butterfly. Her presence brightens a room. She wears a big smile and always shares a warm and welcoming greeting. She shows everyone she meets that she is sincerely happy to meet them. Conversation, beyond small talk, comes naturally to her.

My husband is also a social animal. He loves people. The more people around him, the happier he is. When we walk into a restaurant, I see his eyes scan the room to see if there's anyone he knows. If he recognizes someone, our conversation is immediately put on hold while he hurries over to say hello.

The point? We live within a variety of relationships: in our families, in our circle of friends, in our church homes, in our communities, and at our places of work. Some of us are more comfortable in a broader circle of people than others. Some of us naturally build relationships, while others of us are more cautious and perhaps uncomfortable. Regardless of our personalities or if we are introverts or extroverts, we are *all* called to live in relationship with others, in godly relationships, in relationships filled with love for one another.

What does that look like? What can we do to live out God's love in our relationships with one another?

Let's look at the relationships we might be in. Please allow me to describe the relationships in my life. Maybe my list will be similar to yours.

I'm Wayne's wife and the mother of two adult daughters. I have two sons-in-law. I am my mother's daughter. I am a sister. My two brothers and my sister are each married, so I'm a sister-in-law to their spouses. I am an aunt, a great aunt, and a cousin. I am a friend to some, a neighbor to some, and an acquaintance to many. I am self-employed with no employees. So I have no co-workers, but I have business acquaintances. I have a business network, a personal network, and a social media network. And last but not least, I am a sister in Christ with a family of millions through faith.

There. I've listed the types of relationships I have. However, I don't think the list defines where I am relationally. Where I am relationally depends on each specific relationship. My husband, Wayne, and I are best friends. I look forward to spending time with him every day and miss him when either of us has to travel from home without the other. I share my thoughts, ideas, and dreams with him. Compared to any other relationship I have, he and I are the closest, with the exception of the relationship I have with Jesus.

Each relationship is different, and each relationship evolves over time. Some relationships grow closer, and others grow further apart. For example, we might have a good friend for a time or for a season. Then circumstances change. Perhaps one of us moves, or changes jobs, or gets married, or gets divorced, or has children. The change puts distance between our relationship, weakens it, or ends it over time. Maybe the relationship strengthens for a time, due to shared circumstances. Perhaps we both lost our jobs or one of us turned to the other for help during a stressful period in our lives. Relationships evolve due to changing circumstances.

Relationships also evolve naturally through the passage of

time. Consider my relationship with our daughters. They grew up. As a mom, I had to learn to let them live their own lives as adults. They will say that I haven't quite grasped that concept. I will say that I simply try to help them in the same way I might try to help a close friend. I'm learning that there's a delicate balance between being helpful and interfering.

Some of us have relationships that have soured. This is hardest when it involves someone we loved deeply. There might be a divorce, a daughter who no longer speaks to her mother, or a brother who will have nothing to do with his sister. Sometimes, abusive relationships within families cause them to split forever, even though the concept of a family relationship is still desired. I have a girlfriend whose father and siblings are emotionally abusive to her. Although she intellectually understands that it's better for her to avoid close contact with them, she still wants close family ties. She wants a close, loving family relationship, but her family members don't treat her with love.

I will do what I can, where I am, relationally. It's a delicate balance. One needs to be careful not to become the bull in the china shop of relationships. Yet we need to have the courage to step in or speak up from time to time for the good of the other person, the good of the relationship, or the good of God's kingdom.

How is this done? How do we know what to do, when to do it, when to stop in order to preserve the relationship, and when to proceed at the risk of harming the relationship?

No matter what the relationship, the answer starts with love. We are called to live in God's love and to live out God's love. We are to love others.

What is love?

> *Love is patient, love is kind. It does not envy, it*
> *does not boast, it is not proud. It does not dishonor*

others, it is not self-seeking, it is not easily angered,
it keeps no record of wrongs. Love does not delight
in evil but rejoices with the truth. It always pro-
tects, always trusts, always hopes, always perseveres.
(1 Corinthians 13:4-7)

If I act out of love, I will be patient with those around me. I will wait for them without becoming annoyed or upset. If they make mistakes, I will patiently try to enable them to recognize and correct their mistakes and avoid the same mistakes in the future. I will remain calm when we face difficulties together. From time to time, I may need to exercise forbearance and let an issue drop rather than confront it. Other times, I will exercise calm and persistence, and I won't let the issue drop but will use care not to press too hard too fast. Patience.

I will also show kindness to them. Specifically, I will try to be compassionate and try to understand and empathize with their situation. Perhaps I'll need to ask questions to ensure I understand them and the situation at hand. I will also be considerate in the manner in which I speak to them or treat them and remember to be gentle with my words and benevolent with my actions. I will remember to be thoughtful. Kindness.

I will be careful to avoid dishonoring them. It's important to keep private things private, respect confidentiality, and avoid embarrassing them. I will not expose them to ridicule. I will not gossip. Honor.

I will not be self-seeking in my relationships. My priority must be to first be God-seeking and then work to seek the best for those around me. I will share my time and resources as needed and work toward a cooperative relationship that is mutually viewed as loving. Prior to stepping in or speaking out, I will analyze my own heart and ask, "Am I trying to gain something personally? Am I self-seeking, others-seeking, or God-seeking?" Selfless.

I will check my temper at the door, remain calm, and resist provocation. It's important to present my concerns with tact and avoid the actions or appearance of anger. Instead of listing the history of all wrongs from times past, my focus will be only on the current issue. I will manage current issues in a timely fashion so they don't fester and create a greater likelihood of reacting out of anger. Composed.

In love, I will protect others and keep them and their families safe or away from harm. This may involve loving correction or stepping in urgently on occasion. It might mean taking someone's car keys when they've had too much to drink or confronting someone to end an affair. In love, I will guide them gently toward the Word of God in an effort to protect them from an eternity of regret or hell. Protective.

I will build trust in my relationships and try to be a person whom others can rely on or have confidence in. I will work to be a place of safety, a person of safety. I will strive to live in a manner that reassures others that their concerns, cares, doubts, worries, and questions will not be judged, but will be heard and treated with loving-kindness. Trusting.

Frankly, doing what I can ... living out God's love ... where I am relationally, feels like a lot to remember. I know I've failed in this area many times, perhaps daily, with those I love. Perhaps I've failed the most times with those I hardly know. When have I reached out in friendship to my neighbor, the one I haven't met yet? When I heard an acquaintance was going through a tough time, did I go to her house to see what I might do to help? When I see the prayer list of those in need of healing at church, do I offer to help or send a card? I most often miss the mark, even though I generally know how to treat others with loving-kindness.

I think I'm too busy. The need seems too great. There's always something that needs my attention in my own life. There is always someone, whether an individual, a group, or a cause that needs more help. Do you have similar problems? Do you find yourself so busy trying to keep up with daily life and your own family that reaching out to others is a near impossibility?

I need someone to help me do what I can, where I am, relationally.

Perhaps I'll do better if I picture myself and the other person side by side before Jesus. Neither person is above the other; neither person controls the situation. Then I think of Jesus and his perfect love, his sacrificial love. When I see Jesus in my mind's eye and know that he'll see and hear everything I do and say, it's easier to act out of love toward the person beside me. Maybe this visual works for you too. Maybe you can imagine another situation that will help you live lovingly in your relationships.

In some relationships, there is an element of headship, control, or leadership due to the nature of the relationship. This is the case for a husband and wife, a parent and child, and an employer and employee. In these circumstances, the Bible provides added guidance on what godly relationships look like. They contain an element of mutual respect or love and each person treats the other in a manner that will honor God.

Within our families, women are called to accept their husband's authority and defer to their judgment when there is disagreement, thereby respecting their position as head of the household. I realize that this is somewhat counter-cultural in the United States today. But when we honor and respect our husbands, we honor God. As we live our lives in a godly manner, our husbands may be drawn closer to God through us (1 Peter 3:1-6; Colossians 3:18; Ephesians 5:22). I occasionally respond to my husband irritably or with outbursts of anger, particularly if I'm having a frustrating day. Now, I try to remind myself to treat him kindly and use pleasant words, similar to, or better than, those I speak at church or work. After all, I love him. Shouldn't I treat him well?

The Bible also provides guidance for husbands and how they are to lovingly treat their wives. Husbands are to live in understanding of their wives, honoring and loving them (1 Peter 3:7; Colossians 3:19). The love of a husband toward his wife is to be like the love Jesus has for his church. Jesus gave his life out of love for the church. Husbands are to love their wives as they love themselves. They are to nourish and cherish their wives, just as Jesus nourishes and cherishes his church (Ephesians 5:25-33).

Children are called to obey their parents. Children of all ages, whether young or old, are commanded to honor their parents (Colossians 3:20; Ephesians 6:1-2). We honor God by honoring our parents. At the same time, fathers are admonished not to frustrate, anger, or annoy their children (perhaps through constant scolding or nagging). Instead, fathers are to teach their children about God and train them to live in accordance with God's precepts (Ephesians 6:4).

Finally, workers are expected to obey their employers, treat those in authority with respect, and conduct themselves as though they are working for the Lord. In the same manner, employers are to treat their workers with respect and are not to threaten them. All people are to work wholeheartedly as though for God himself (Ephesians 6:5-9).

> *Finally, all of you, be like-minded, be sympathetic, love one another, be compassionate and humble. Do not repay evil with evil or insult with insult. On the contrary, repay evil with blessing, because to this you were called so that you may inherit a blessing.*
> (1 Peter 3:8-9)

We are called to live out God's love in all of our relationships and be a blessing to others. Since recognizing this call, I have made a conscious effort to live out God's love in all encounters with others. As an introvert, I found this very hard to do in the beginning. In fact, I wasn't quite sure what to do. So after giving it some thought, I decided that I could simply practice good and helpful manners. I held the door for others, let someone else go first in a line, and smiled whether I was personally happy or not. At first it felt awkward (almost like the smile I used with the new girl on the bus), but soon I was pleasantly surprised at how many smiles I received in return.

Over time, I got brave enough to offer a simple greeting and even add a comment about the weather. I now voice to others that I like their clothing, hair, or car rather than only thinking about it as I walk past. The people I have encountered typically respond kindly. They chat with me, offer to help me, and more. A simple smile has made me more approachable and enabled others to open up their hearts to me and share their joys and sorrows. My effort to live out God's love with a simple smile has blessed *me*, a truly unexpected result. I am happier now than ever before.

Do you want to know something else? Now, I intentionally put on a smile before I answer the telephone. People can hear the smile! Try it. Try to sound tired or grumpy while your face dons a smile. It can't be done.

Several years ago, when I worked full-time and our daughters were in middle school, I came home from work, and our older daughter was at a friend's home. This was unusual for her, so I asked our after-school caregiver what was going on. After much prodding, she told me that our daughter wanted to talk to a mom and she didn't want to bother me at work.

I replied, with hurt feelings, "But I've always told her she can call anytime."

The caregiver responded, "I know that's what you told her, but that's not how you sound when you answer the phone."

It was a tough lesson.

Remember the story of Mary and Martha? When Jesus visited their home, Martha worked very hard to be a good hostess and busied herself in the kitchen. She became frustrated with Mary because Mary didn't help her. Instead, Mary focused her attention on Jesus and her relationship with him. When Martha complained, Jesus told her that Mary had made the right choice (Luke 10:38-42). It's the relationship that counts.

Since that experience with my daughter, I have worked to remember that relationships are more important than work. There will always be more work to do. But when someone is in need, I find time in my busy schedule and give them one of the greatest gifts: time. Spending time, giving time, and making time for others out of loving-kindness is what counts.

The work, chores, and busyness should often wait. However, it's a difficult challenge in this day of ever-increasing demands for productivity. It's also a challenge to give your undivided attention to the person in your presence as compared to the text message or phone call that is interrupting your conversation. To act out of loving-kindness and respect, to properly discern the greater need at the time, *and* to meet your obligations to others (such as to your employer, customers, or family) is often a difficult balance to maintain.

Pray. Ask God to give you discernment when you struggle with this balance. Try to be the person who God wants you to be all the time and seek the help of the Holy Spirit. As you draw closer to God, he draws closer to you. Then you will sense his prodding hand as he guides you in your daily encounters with others. Pray regularly. Ask God to enable you to be a reflection of Jesus so when people interact with you, they will know and feel Jesus' love.

As mentioned earlier, I pray that God will enable others to see Jesus' love when they see me. Perhaps with this prayer, God will govern my behavior, my thoughts, my words, and my time. Perhaps he will open doors to a safe and loving conversation with someone in need or alter my schedule so I have time to lend a helping hand. It's an easy prayer to remember. It's an easy prayer to say throughout the day.

Try it. Say this prayer every day throughout your day, perhaps each time you get out of your car. Remember this prayer when you are angry with someone or trying to resolve a conflict. If you're a person who likes to keep a journal, make a note of the prayer and your personal encounters throughout the day. I'm certain you will find unexpected surprises.

> *Therefore, I urge you, brothers and sisters, in view of God's mercy, to offer your bodies as a living sacrifice, holy and pleasing to God—this is your true and proper worship.* (Romans 12:1)

With God's love in my life, to live out God's love, where I am, in my relationships, is becoming a more natural part of my life, even for me – an introvert at heart. I have shared God's love with a simple smile and no longer need to know someone well before I'll talk with him or her. Through God's love in my life, I can bless others. In return, they bless me and God blesses me.

Live out God's love wherever you are relationally, whether the person is your friend, foe, family member, neighbor, stranger, pre-believer in Jesus, or brother or sister in Christ. As you do, God will place you around those who need a loving response, a kind word, an act of kindness, godly advice, a soft shoulder, or a helping hand. When God places you with someone in need, respond out of God's love. As others see Jesus and his love through you, you will also see more of Jesus in your life.

I will do what I can, where I am – relationally. Will you do what you can to share God's love in your relationships?

I Will Do What I Can, Where I Am, With I AM!

Chapter 14

I Can Where I Am – Emotionally

"No, you don't get it. You don't know how I feel!"

"I wish I had someone to talk to who understands what I'm going through."

"You've never had this happen to you, so how could you possibly understand?"

"I don't know how to explain it. The feeling never goes away."

"I'm worthless. Who could love me now?"

"I'm damaged goods. No one would ever want to marry someone like me."

"How can I ever move forward after the death of my daughter?"

"I worry all the time about him. I am so afraid that he will never come home."

Have you said anything like this before? Have you been overcome with feelings of worry, heartbreak, fear, grief, regret, shame, or guilt? Have you faced some sort of devastating event in your life that you struggled to overcome?

Maybe you lost a child or grieved over a miscarriage. Maybe you've struggled to overcome the aftermath of emotional, physical, or sexual abuse. Perhaps you made a regrettable choice in your past that has damaged your emotional well-being through unresolved guilt and shame. Perhaps you've lost your sense of self-worth or self-confidence as a result of extended unemployment. Maybe you've had to face a debilitating accident or disease and struggled to find joy in your life. In a tough economy, maybe you lost your home to foreclosure.

What hardships have you faced in your past? Have you recovered from them? Have you forgiven those who were involved in or caused the problem? Do you know God's love and forgiveness? Have you found Jesus' touch of healing? Maybe you've tried to bury the past, only to have it rear its ugly head at the most inopportune moments and cause you to well up in tears, explode in anger, or retreat into solitude.

When I wrote my second book, *Grapple with Guilt, Shed the Shame*, I wanted to bring the subject to life by using real-life stories of people who have struggled with a sense of guilt or shame in their lives. So I solicited real-life stories through my many e-mail contacts. To my dismay, I discovered that the world we live in is a very sick world. The things I heard that fathers did to their daughters, siblings did to each other, husbands did to their wives, and friends did to each other shocked and dismayed me. Instead of love for one another, I heard stories of destruction, hate, anger, and fear.

Some of the people who shared their stories had found healing in Christ Jesus. Others were still in the process of healing. And for some, when they shared their story with me, it was the first time ever that they let go of their deepest life secret. They took their first step toward healing when they talked with me.

Therefore confess your sins to each other and pray

*for each other so that you may be healed. The prayer
of a righteous person is powerful and effective.*
(James 5:16)

For those who still struggle emotionally, please know you
can give all your concerns and worries to God. God loves you.
Through Jesus, you can be healed. *Cast all your anxiety on him
because he cares for you* (1 Peter 5:7).

Jesus is the Great Healer. He healed people with a touch of
his hand. His healing powers went out when people touched his
robe. He healed people by simply stating that they were healed,
and forgave their sins in addition to healing their physical bodies. He freed them from demons and even raised people from
the dead. He listened to those who needed healing and healed
not only their physical bodies but also their emotional state.
Whatever you're going through now or have faced in the past,
seek Jesus. He will listen. Through him you can be healed.

*The LORD hears his people when they call to him
for help. He rescues them from all their troubles.
The LORD is close to the brokenhearted; he rescues those whose spirits are crushed. The righteous
person faces many troubles, but the LORD comes
to the rescue each time. For the LORD protects the
bones of the righteous; not one of them is broken!*
(Psalm 34:17-20 NLT)

Why do I bring up our heartbreaks in a book about living
out God's love? God uses our brokenness for good things. The
apostle Paul, in Romans 8:28, states, *And we know that in all
things God works for the good of those who love him, who have
been called according to his purpose.* God calls us to live out
his love by loving others. God *comforts us in all our troubles,
so that we can comfort those in any trouble with the comfort we
ourselves receive from God* (2 Corinthians1:4).

Carry each other's burdens. (Galatians 6:2)

When someone is hurting or facing a devastating issue in life, who can empathize better than a person who truly understands the issue? It helps to share our troubles, worries, and fears with someone who has been there and done that, someone who understands the issues and feelings, having gone through a similar personal experience. Conversely, it's often offensive when suffering a serious loss (for example, the death of a loved one) to hear the words, "I know just how you feel," from a person who hasn't struggled with the loss of a loved one. In some circumstances, until one has personal experience with a similar issue, he or she cannot truly understand the pain of another. One can't imagine the hurt and depth of loss.

From time to time, I'm called to share my personal experiences of living in the aftermath of abortion at pregnancy center fundraisers, pro-life rallies, and workshops intended to help other post-abortive women find the path of forgiveness and emotional healing.

Invariably, at the end of one of these events, a woman will whisper in my ear, "I've never told anyone this before, but I've been in your same shoes. Thank you for sharing. Your words have been a great help."

These women have discovered a safe place for their confession, a place with someone who has been on the same or a similar path. God can and does use our experiences to help others get through their current situations.

God can and will use our personal experiences to help others if we are willing to be a safe "place" for others, a safe person of empathy, openness, and compassion. Be a person who will listen, pray, and provide guidance when requested, someone who doesn't judge, yet speaks God's truth.

Have you ever wondered why Mary traveled a distance that

is believed to be up to eighty miles to visit her cousin Elizabeth upon hearing from the angel that Elizabeth, in her old age, was pregnant? Elizabeth was about six months' pregnant when Mary arrived. I've tried to put myself in Mary's shoes. The same angel had just told Mary that she too would become pregnant, even though she was a virgin. Maybe Mary wanted to verify the truth of the angel's words, thinking that if Elizabeth was indeed pregnant, she could trust that she truly had been visited by an angel. Maybe Mary was afraid about how she would tell Joseph, or was fearful for her future, fearful of the unknown. *What would Joseph do? Would she be accused and then ostracized by her community? Joseph could choose to have her stoned to death. What would her family do? What would her life be like? How does she trust God and remain faithful to her promise when she is so frightened?*

Perhaps Mary believed Elizabeth would be a safe person with whom she could share her questions, concerns, and fears. Perhaps Mary hoped Elizabeth would have wisdom to share, being also a woman bearing a child miraculously. Maybe Mary needed a safe place to tell her story about the angel and her pregnancy before she faced Joseph and all the people in her own community.

Mary stayed with Elizabeth about three months. The Bible doesn't tell us why. Maybe Mary stayed long enough to know for certain that she was indeed pregnant or she wanted to observe Elizabeth's pregnancy. Perhaps, being pregnant at a vintage age, Elizabeth simply needed extra help with the household chores so she could get adequate rest. While Elizabeth likely helped Mary emotionally and spiritually, Mary may have helped Elizabeth physically.

We don't know for certain what Mary and Elizabeth did or discussed during Mary's three-month visit. But their likely relationship is an excellent example of how we might be called to use our personal experiences to help others.

God understands our need to know that others can relate to our lives. He chose to relate to each of us on a personal level, through the earthly experiences of Jesus. Jesus faced temptation in the desert, disrespect and criticism from his own community, and grief and sorrow following the death of his friend Lazarus. Jesus faced false accusations, hatred, and condemnation. He faced pain when his closest friends betrayed him, denied him, and abandoned him. He faced humiliation on the road, carrying his cross, and being stripped and beaten. Finally, he faced the extraordinary physical pain of death through crucifixion.

For we do not have a high priest who is unable to empathize with our weaknesses, but we have one who has been tempted in every way, just as we are—yet he did not sin. (Hebrews 4:15)

Jesus knows and understands what we face in our daily lives. Through Jesus' earthly life, God himself experienced life on earth, life in a broken world, life as we might know it. God understands how we feel when we face the trials, joys, and heartbreaks of life on earth. Since we know that God understands, we also know that we can freely go to him, give him our burdens, and find comfort, encouragement, security, and love.

It's through Christ's example and the example of Mary and Elizabeth that we're encouraged to live out God's love by doing what we can where we are emotionally.

How is that done?

Do you remember the days when people advertised their business by having an employee wear a sandwich board with their business advertisement printed on the front and the back, and walk along the city sidewalk? Maybe you've seen it in old movies. The sandwich board consisted of two large sheets of cardboard or thin wooden boards held together with straps that rested on the shoulders of the person and sandwiched them between the two boards. I occasionally imagine what people see on my imaginary sandwich board when they meet me. Most often, I try to limit the view to only the front board. On the front board, I present all of the wonderful aspects of my life, perhaps with just a little exaggeration. Conversely, I try to hide the backboard. On the backboard, the poor choices of my past, along with my current struggles, are written. I'd prefer people didn't know about those things.

However, if I only present a picture-perfect life, others will never know that I might truly understand how they feel about some of the struggles they may be facing. If I allow people to know the real me – the human, less-than-perfect, sinful, and occasionally struggling me – I then become a safe place for them. Fortunately, it's not necessary to wear all of this information on a sandwich board. To become a safe place, a helpful place for others, it's often only necessary to share your story at the right time and place. Keep an outward focus, a focus on love for the person with whom you share your story.

I know that because of my willingness to share my story, I have opened the door for many women to unburden their hearts. Through my books and speaking engagements, many women have heard my story of regrettable teenage choices that resulted in an untimely pregnancy and the death of my baby through abortion. Because of my openness and transparency, I have become a safe place for women to go with their own stories of regrettable choices and life in the aftermath of those choices.

I have opened myself to vulnerability. Yet at the same time, I found freedom through Jesus and his love and grace-filled forgiveness. As I open my life's heartbreak to others, I am able to live out God's love toward others and help them take steps toward their own healing through Christ Jesus.

God is able to use our brokenness for good.

What experiences have you had that make you a safe, approachable person, a person of compassion, understanding, and wisdom? Where are you emotionally with these experiences? Are you ready and able to use your experiences to help others?

- Have you suffered with unresolved guilt and shame based on something you've done?
- Are you a cancer survivor?
- Have you suffered the pain and grief of one or more miscarriages?
- Are you divorced?
- Are you estranged from one of your adult children?
- Have you endured the loss of a child?
- Were you a single parent who juggled all the family's needs by yourself?
- Have you faced job loss or struggled financially?
- Perhaps you're a recovering drug addict or alcoholic?
- Have you been a long-term caregiver for an aging parent or someone with special needs?

This is only a partial list. If you've found strength, healing, courage, comfort, and love through Jesus during times such as these, you might be the safe person that someone else needs. The cliché is, "Misery loves company." It's not that misery wants company to wallow in the pain. Misery needs company so that one can be lifted up in hope and healing through the name of Jesus.

> *Not only so, but we also glory in our sufferings,*
> *because we know that suffering produces persever-*
> *ance; perseverance, character; and character, hope.*
> (Romans 5:3-4)

Consider allowing others to catch a glimpse of the back of your sandwich board, particularly if you become aware of their similar but current struggle. You can privately open the door to conversation or make your experiences known to your church pastor or leaders. Let them know that if they learn of someone who could use a compassionate and empathic ear to listen, along with a soft shoulder to lean on, you might be just the right person.

I will do what I can, where I am – emotionally. I will allow God to use my past brokenness to help others find Christ's love. If I can help someone find hope in this life by sharing my personal story and the ultimate love and healing touch of Christ, I will share it.

Will you do what you can where you are emotionally?

I Will Do What I Can, Where I Am, With I AM!

Chapter 15

I Can Where I Am – Spiritually

I know a young man, someone close to us, who doesn't share the same level of faith in Jesus that my husband and I share. He carries with him doubts and questions. He finds the Bible to be in conflict with many of the teachings he has learned in our public school systems, because of his particular interest and focus on science. Our schools teach that the scientific theory of evolution is more than just a theory, and they close the door to all other discussions.

It's not always easy to overcome these teachings, particularly when one has been taught about this so-called scientific fact throughout his or her entire educational life.

> *The person without the Spirit does not accept the things that come from the Spirit of God but considers them foolishness, and cannot understand them because they are discerned only through the Spirit.*
> (1 Corinthians 2:14)

Out of deep concern for this young man and his family's eternal future, my husband and I had a heart-to-heart discussion with him about our faith. I was worried about the discussion, because I recognized the importance of the topic coupled with a concern that we might push him away from Jesus rather than draw him toward Jesus. I felt so spiritually inadequate to have that discussion. By that time, I had written five Christian books and read the Bible through five times, including the footnotes and commentaries contained within my printed copies. I immersed myself in numerous Christian books of all types: fiction, non-fiction, novels, biographies, self-help, and more. Even the Certificate in Equipping I earned from The Master's Institute didn't seem to bolster my confidence level for the conversation.

I think I'm reasonably well versed in my intellectual knowledge of God's Word, although I know that knowledge isn't all there is. A relationship with God is critical to one's spiritual well-being and growth. I discovered and entered into a relationship with God at thirty-eight years old. Yet even after I had experienced a relationship with God for over fifteen years, I still worried about our conversation about faith with this young man.

I will do what I can, where I am – spiritually.

I don't see a requirement in the above sentence that says I need to be an expert in the spiritual arena to do what I can. It doesn't say I have to be an ordained pastor, have a degree in theology, a master's of divinity, or any other formal credentials to do what I can, where I am, spiritually.

> *"When you are brought before synagogues, rulers and authorities, do not worry about how you will defend yourselves or what you will say, for the Holy Spirit will teach you at that time what you should say."* (Luke 12:11-12)

When God called Moses to go to Egypt and convince Pharaoh to free the Israelites, *Moses said to the Lord, "Pardon*

your servant, Lord. I have never been eloquent, neither in the
past nor since you have spoken to your servant. I am slow of
speech and tongue."

The LORD *said to him, "Who gave human beings their mouths?*
Who makes them deaf or mute? Who gives them sight or makes
them blind? Is it not I, the LORD*? Now go; I will help you speak*
and will teach you what to say" (Exodus 4:10-12). God said he
would provide Moses with the words he needed. God said to
Moses, just go, do what you can, and I'll provide.

God will provide for each of us as well, if we just do what
we can and trust him to do the rest. It doesn't matter if you're
new to your faith or if you've been walking with the Lord for
many years. What matters is that you do what you can where
you are spiritually. Recognize and admit your potential limitations, whether they are knowledge limitations, educational
limitations, or spiritual maturity limitations. Then, give those
limitations to God and do what you can from your strengths.
Often it's most effective to simply explain how you came to
believe in Jesus. The Holy Spirit frequently uses our personal
stories – our testimonies about our faith journeys – to open
the hearts of pre-believers.

> *Now these are the gifts Christ gave to the church:*
> *the apostles, the prophets, the evangelists, and the*
> *pastors and teachers. Their responsibility is to equip*
> *God's people to do his work and build up the church,*
> *the body of Christ. This will continue until we all*
> *come to such unity in our faith and knowledge*
> *of God's Son that we will be mature in the Lord,*
> *measuring up to the full and complete standard of*
> *Christ.* (Ephesians 4:11-13 NLT)

The Bible tells us that God, through his Holy Spirit, gives
each of us certain gifts or strengths according to our purpose.

Not all people receive the same gifts and strengths, and not all gifts and strengths are given to us in the same degree. As a result, we as the church are able to reach out broadly, work together as one body in Christ, and build up the church according to our individual callings and our individual purposes, the purposes for each of our lives as determined by God (1 Corinthians 12:7-14, 27-31). With the gifts and strengths he gives us, we can do what we can, and the Lord will give us all we need to act in accordance with his specific call on our lives.

Maybe it's not ability that concerns you. Maybe you're concerned about worthiness. For example, I've made many mistakes, some of which I previously believed were unforgiveable and caused me to feel shame and embarrassment. I believed the lie that I was unworthy for any godly purpose. I believed I was not spiritually ready or worthy to reach out to others and have a positive impact on the kingdom of heaven.

Does this sound familiar? Do you feel unworthy or lacking in some way?

Consider the prophet Isaiah and his vision described in Isaiah 6. In his vision, Isaiah found himself in the highest temple of God. After he observed angels praising God, he saw the glory of God fill the temple with holiness. The vision was so great, the holiness of God so overwhelming, that Isaiah instantly recognized his personal unworthiness to be in the presence of God. He exclaimed, *"I am ruined! For I am a man of unclean lips, and I live among a people of unclean lips, and my eyes have seen the King, the LORD Almighty"* (Isaiah 6:5).

At that, one of the angels picked up a burning coal from the altar and touched Isaiah's lips, saying, *"See, this has touched your lips; your guilt is taken away and your sin atoned for."* By this, Isaiah's sin was taken away. Isaiah, once unworthy for God's call, was now able to respond affirmatively when God asked, *"Whom shall I send?"* Isaiah resoundingly responded, *"Here am I. Send me!"* (Isaiah 6:6-8).

Isaiah exclaimed, "Send me!" He was first unworthy because of his sinfulness, but was then made worthy through God's grace.

We can't make ourselves worthy of God's call on our lives. But that has never stopped God. God knows all about our unworthiness, mistakes, and sins. But through the death and resurrection of Jesus, through God's grace and mercy, our sins have been forgiven. Faith in Jesus alone makes us worthy to respond to God's call on our lives. God will purify us and make us ready. God used Moses, a murderer. He used Rahab, a prostitute. They said yes to God's call, and that's all we need to say now.

All we have to do is to respond, "Here I am, Lord. Send me! Use me! I am available. I want to help. I will do what I can where I am!"

Listen for his call.

Sometimes God will call us to action for a day or moment in time when someone needs a prayer, hug, kind word, or smile. These are expressions of God's love from our hearts. Other times he will call us to a particular job for a season. We may be called to minister to someone as they face an illness or struggle with faith questions. Our special gifts may be called on to lead a Bible study at church or influence the spiritual lives of the children in our families or extended families. God might call some of us to do what we can as a lifetime commitment through our chosen professions. He might call some to care for a developmentally or physically challenged family member. Others he might call to serve their church communities or serve their neighbors through local, state, or federal governments with leadership skills founded upon biblical truths and teachings.

I will seek God's wisdom and trust him to provide what I need when I need it.

Perhaps you still think like Moses: *Surely there is someone who can do more than I, or there is someone who can do this job better than I.* Perhaps you feel inadequate for the conversation that you're about to hold with someone about the reasons for your faith. I encourage you not to worry. There's much you can do. Each of us who walks with the Lord is blessed with gifts of grace (divine influence upon our hearts) and the fruit of his Holy Spirit.

> *But to each one of us grace has been given as Christ apportioned it.* (Ephesians 4:7)

When in doubt, rely on God and the gifts of grace he gives to each of us to enable us to do works of service. What are the gifts of grace? They are the spiritual gifts that enable us to respond to God's call. God might bless one of us with a gift of wisdom, knowledge, or teaching. He might bless another with a gift of prophesy or healing. We don't need to worry about our ability or inability to answer God's call on our lives. We only need to do what we can and trust God for the necessary gifts of grace. God will bless us with what we need for each circumstance.

> *But the fruit of the Spirit is love, joy, peace, forbearance, kindness, goodness, faithfulness, gentleness and self-control. Against such things there is no law.* (Galatians 5:22-23)

Additionally, we can exhibit the fruit of the Spirit throughout our daily lives. Through the Spirit, we can love those around us, including those who are hard to love. Our lives exhibit joy, the kind of joy that comes only from Christ. In obedience, we live with a sense of peace and contentedness regardless of our circumstances. We are patient and wait on the Lord during times of difficulty. Kindness flows from us even when others don't seem to be deserving of our kindness. Our lives are a model of goodness and fairness in business and in our daily tasks. We exhibit faithfulness and trustworthiness when we show ourselves to be reliable and true to our word. As the Spirit flows through us, he brings gentleness to all, including in the midst of potentially explosive or highly emotional situations. And in a world of excess, our lives demonstrate and exercise self-control over our behaviors, tempers, and habits.

How did our conversation go with our young friend? It went well. Did we bring him to faith in Christ Jesus? Not in that conversation. But we did what we could and trust that God will take it from here.

I will do what I can. I will rely heavily on the gifts of grace and on the fruits of the Holy Spirit. Through faith, the gifts of the Holy Spirit, and the fruit of the Holy Spirit, I will do what I can, where I am – spiritually. God will prepare me.

I Will Do What I Can, Where I Am, With I AM!

Chapter 16

I Can Where I Am – Financially

I'm so thankful for caller ID on my telephone. It's one of the best inventions of all time. My phone seems to ring endlessly. I signed up for the Do Not Call Registry. So, in theory, I'm not supposed to receive any calls from salespeople. Well, I think it's working. I don't recall any unsolicited calls from salespeople recently. But I get numerous calls per day from political and charitable organizations seeking money. The alumni associations for the schools my husband and I attended, and the schools our daughters attended also call from time to time. Everyone needs more money.

Thanks to caller ID, I now avoid most of the calls by simply not answering the phone.

But then I get my mail. I don't know how the U.S. Postal Service operates in the red. They must give too great a discount on all of the junk mail I receive. It seems that about 75 percent of my mail is from political organizations seeking money. Another 10 percent of my mail comes from charitable organizations seeking money. The next 10 percent comprises mail order catalogues. The rest is what I consider real mail: bills, cards, and letters. My mail averages about ten items per day. In a year, my mail alone – unsolicited mail – probably destroys a small forest. Most of the senders request my financial support. Everyone needs more money.

Additional people and organizations that seem to be in constant need of money include our church; the local youth group; the volunteer fire department; our federal, state, and local governments seeking tax dollars; community projects; and various high school sports teams, band members, choir members, and other school organizations.

My bank account is not an ever-flowing river of cash. It has its limits. The money only goes so far. My bank account is more like the sprinkling can I use to water our plants. It starts out strong on payday. That's when I cover the most essential expenses, the plants that are drooping with thirst. Then, as the sprinkling can lightens, I pour out the water more gingerly, so each plant gets a little, until I watch the last little trickle barely moisten the dirt and the checkbook is dry. I'd love to refill the sprinkling can of money, but I have to wait until payday. Actually, I have to wait until my husband's payday. It's a good thing one of us has a regular, paying job.

When I was about thirty years old, I worked as an attorney for a major oil company in Houston, Texas. During lunch one day, I and a few other attorneys went for a walk to enjoy the beautiful weather. While we walked, the discussion turned to family budgets, the cost of new cars, and the prices of homes in the area. One of the attorneys, Milton, stated that he and his family tithed. They gave one-tenth of their income to God through their church.

One-tenth, a tithe. I pondered that amount silently. That's a lot of money. I recalled that the Bible said the Israelites were to give one-tenth of their grain, cattle, and other forms of earnings to God, but I didn't know if I needed or even wanted to do so. Wayne and I had just started our family. We recently bought a house and had a ton of student loans. *Tithe? I don't think so. No one really does that, do they? Does Milton really give that much to church?*

> *"Bring the whole tithe into the storehouse, that there may be food in my house. Test me in this," says the* Lord *Almighty, "and see if I will not throw open the floodgates of heaven and pour out so much bless- ing that there will not be room enough to store it."*
> (Malachi 3:10)

"We're a young family. We have three kids and can't afford higher taxes. So we voted against the school referendum," said the young mother whose children weren't in school yet. She spoke without knowledge that classes were overcrowded and some were held in small, windowless rooms originally intended to be storage closets.

"Both my neighbor and his wife lost their jobs. I wonder how they're getting by. I'm so glad that we're not in their boat. Hopefully, unemployment payments are enough to get them by," said the woman who believed it's the government's respon- sibility to help those in need, while she was failing to offer help to her neighbor.

> *Do not withhold good from those to whom it is due, when it is in your power to act. Do not say to your neighbor, "Come back tomorrow and I'll give it to you"— when you already have it with you.*
> (Proverbs 3:27-28)

"My grandparents always donated five dollars to church each week. My parents did the same amount. So, sure, that amount seems right. That's what we'll donate," said the young man to his wife, as they returned to church after a several-year hiatus. He didn't think about the difference in value of the five dollars given by his grandparents compared to the value of five dollars in today's terms.

"I thought about tithing to church, but then I lost my job. There's no money left after we pay the basic bills. We had to cut out all donations to all organizations."

> *This is what the LORD Almighty says: "Give careful thought to your ways. Go up into the mountains and bring down timber and build my house, so that I may take pleasure in it and be honored," says the LORD. "You expected much, but see, it turned out to be little. What you brought home, I blew away. Why?" declares the LORD Almighty. "Because of my house, which remains a ruin, while each of you is busy with your own house." (Haggai 1:7-9)*

"We were finally able to buy a house. Now we're saving to get a new car and trying to build a college fund for our kids. There's nothing left to donate. Oh, we agree, it's a very good cause, but we need a few more years to get on our feet. Then we can be more generous," explained the young professional couple. "On top of all that, do you have any idea how much daycare costs these days? And Alisha starts school next year. We were shocked to learn what the tuition will be at her private school."

> *Whoever is kind to the poor lends to the LORD,*
> *and he will reward them for what they have done.*
> (Proverbs 19:17)

The sprinkling can of money runs dry no matter who we are or what our circumstances are. (Well, okay. Maybe that's not true for Bill Gates or some others with extreme wealth. But for the rest of us, that's how life works.) Sometimes we face adversity and cut into our budgets. On occasion, we stretch our budgets too far, because we believe that we deserve a new car or need an extra bedroom in our apartment. Sometimes we dream bigger than our current incomes can support. We often put our own dreams and needs above those in greater need. It's easy to forget that all that we have – our jobs, our homes, our food, our clothing, and our money – comes from God. When we die, we will leave all these things behind. They aren't ours to keep. God gave them to us and he expects us to be good stewards of his provision.

> *"Give, and it will be given to you. A good measure, pressed down, shaken together and running over, will be poured into your lap. For with the measure you use, it will be measured to you."* (Luke 6:38)

Good stewards of his provision? What does that mean?

I will do what I can, where I am – financially. What can I do? Can I or should I do more than I am? Shouldn't I first provide for my family's needs? Isn't it okay to get some of the things we would like to have beyond our basic needs? I work hard. I want some extras. I deserve some extras. Right?

> *Why spend money on what is not bread, and your labor on what does not satisfy? Listen, listen to me, and eat what is good, and you will delight in the richest of fare.* (Isaiah 55:2)

Maybe you're right, and you do deserve some extras. Maybe God has already blessed you with many extras or taken away some of your extras. Maybe you're still waiting for your fair share of extras. But the point here is simply that it's not about you. It's about God.

> *Take delight in the LORD, and he will give you the desires of your heart.* (Psalm 37:4)

The Bible has so much to say about money that Randy Alcorn wrote an entire book about it, a book I recommend to each of you. It's called *Money, Possessions and Eternity*, published by Tyndale House Publishers, Inc. My words here can't possibly cover all there is to say about money and God's expectations regarding how we are to use it. So I'll simplify it here. All we need and all we want starts first with God. With him, we can do what we can where we are financially, and what we can do is more than we might ever imagine.

> *"Do not store up for yourselves treasures on earth, where moths and vermin destroy, and where thieves break in and steal. But store up for yourselves treasures in heaven, where moths and vermin do not destroy, and where thieves do not break in and steal. For where your treasure is, there your heart will be also."* (Matthew 6:19-21)

In 2003, I finally responded to God's call on my life. He called me to leave my paid employment, my career as I knew it, and one-half of our family's income. Since March of 2001, he had been telling me, *"No one can serve two masters. Either you will hate the one and love the other, or you will be devoted to the one and despise the other. You cannot serve both God and money"* (Matthew 6:24). It seemed everywhere I looked, there was that message. It was there when I watched an evangelist on television, when I read the Bible, in one of my favorite Christian books, and in the message from our pastor at church on Sunday. Over and over and over, *You cannot serve both God and money.*

I argued with God in my prayers. "You can't be serious, God. I need my job. How will we meet our bills? Our bills are set based on two incomes. Sure, maybe we could get by with less, but I don't *want* to get by with less. I like my lifestyle. People will think I'm crazy, or that I'm a failure." The message came again, *You cannot serve both God and money.*

> *Whoever loves money never has enough; whoever loves wealth is never satisfied with their income. This too is meaningless.* (Ecclesiastes 5:10)

I left my job.

My husband and I went to our financial advisor and told him we didn't have enough money to meet our bills. We told him a dollar amount that we needed to make ends meet, a minimum amount that we would need. The budget was going to be tight. He provided ideas on how we might restructure our finances to accomplish our needs. Three days later, God blessed us with an unexpected sum of money, just enough to provide for our budgetary gap for six months.

I answered God's call affirmatively, albeit reluctantly at best. He provided. I did what I could where I was financially. I did what I believed wasn't possible. By the world's measure, I did what I thought was harmful to my family's financial well-being and certainly harmful to my personal sense of pride and success. I, and my husband, did what God called us to do, and God provided.

I did what I could, but what I did pales in comparison to what others have done.

Some people are wealthy. It's easy for them to donate to church or charities with large amounts of money from their surplus. Others have barely enough to support themselves and their families, maybe not even that much. One day, Jesus sat across from the temple treasury with his disciples. As he watched the people drop money into the treasury, he noticed as the wealthy put in large sums. Then a poor widow came to give her offering. Into the treasury she dropped all that she had – two small coins.

Jesus noted the poor widow's gift to the temple treasury and said to his disciples, *"Truly I tell you, this poor widow has put more into the treasury than all the others. They all gave out of their wealth; but she, out of her poverty, put in everything—all she had to live on"* (Mark 12:43b-44). The widow gave all she had to live on.

I've never done that. I once thought that to tithe would be a substantial gift. It seemed that giving 10 percent was more than I could afford. However, I've learned that the more I give, the less I miss. Yet I've never tested the concept to the point of giving my all, or even giving a substantial portion of my wealth.

Do you think the poor widow went hungry that evening? The Bible doesn't specifically tell us, but I don't think she did.

In 1 Kings 17, there's a story about a widow and her son who lived in Zarephath. They had only enough grain and oil for one more meal. There had been no rain in the land for a very long time. At God's direction, Elijah went to Zarephath. God told Elijah that he had commanded a widow to provide for him there. When Elijah arrived at the city gate, he saw the widow as she collected wood to use for baking the last of her bread. Elijah called to her and asked her for a cup of water and a piece of bread. She told Elijah that she only had enough for a final meal for her and her son. Elijah told her not to be afraid and to bring him a small loaf, because God would provide for her. Specifically, he said, *"For this is what the LORD, the God of Israel, says: 'The jar of flour will not be used up and the jug of oil will not run dry until the day the LORD sends rain on the land'"* (1 Kings 17:14). The widow did as Elijah asked, and her flour jar and oil jug did not run empty.

The widow prepared to give all she had and trusted in God through his word spoken through Elijah.

If someone came to your house, in critical need, would you give all you have? Would I? I've never been asked to give all I have. Would I trust in God's provision in that matter?. I don't know what I'd do. I'm afraid I'd want to give only from my surplus, or maybe a little more than that. But give all that I have? Lord God, if you expect me to do that, I pray that you make your request clear and bless me with the faith of these two widows to trust in your total provision.

Listen for God's call. Maybe you'll be called to share a casserole with your unemployed neighbor each week. You might be called to forego some profit, and, in so doing, create a new opportunity for another. If you have more time than money, God might ask you to volunteer and support a good cause. Is God asking you to put your trust in him to provide for your financial needs?

> *Remember this: Whoever sows sparingly will also reap sparingly, and whoever sows generously will also reap generously. Each of you should give what you have decided in your heart to give, not reluctantly or under compulsion, for God loves a cheerful giver. And God is able to bless you abundantly, so that in all things at all times, having all that you need, you will abound in every good work.*
> (2 Corinthians 9:6-8)

Pray for clarity and his guidance. If you're sure you're stepping forward with God, with the Great I AM, in accordance with his plan for you, trust him. God will provide when you respond positively to his call.

Seek God first. Notice, recognize, and empathize with the needs of those around you, your neighbors. God will enable you to do what you can and much more, if you place your trust in him.

I will do what I can, where I am – financially – whether I'm wealthy or poor. What will you choose to do?

I Will Do What I Can, Where I Am, With I AM!

Chapter 17

I Can with I AM

I will do what I can, where I am, with I AM.

With I AM? Does God need my help?

God doesn't need our help, because he's all powerful. But he wants us to join him. During Jesus' ministry, he taught about the kingdom of God throughout many towns and villages. He saw the crowds and that they were hurting in many ways: economically, physically, and spiritually. He had compassion on them. Jesus told his disciples, *"The harvest is plentiful but the workers are few"* (Matthew 9:37). The harvest is plentiful. The need is great. We, as workers during harvest, can make a difference. We can see the need and have compassion, as Jesus did.

The issues are endless. There are people in financial need, people who aren't well physically, people who suffer from mental illness, people who are incarcerated, people who are victims of crime, people who are abused by others, people who are unemployed, people who are homeless, and people who believe they have no worth.

There are people who don't believe in God, people who have never heard of God, and people who are confused by the wide variety of spiritual messages proposed as truth throughout our nation, a nation that promotes acceptance of all spiritual beliefs.

Many of our nation's leaders are power hungry, lack moral values, fail to act for the greater good, and look out only for the good of themselves or their political party. As a nation, we struggle with corruption, crime, drug addiction, lost family values, and a loss of our foundational moral fabric. Our courts have successfully removed prayer from our schools. Atheist groups fight to remove God from our language, history, and all public forums. Millions of unborn babies are killed in the name of women's health care rights.

Our world is in havoc. Christians are persecuted, rockets are flying, nations are attempting to take over other nations, and terrorist groups are gaining power.

It breaks my heart, frightens me, and overwhelms me. I fear for the future of our daughters and their future families. I fear for the future on earth for your sons and daughters, your grandchildren and great-grandchildren.

The harvest is plentiful. The needs are great. And the workers are few.

What can I do? What can you do? Is there anything any one person can do? Where do we start?

> *For God is working in you, giving you the*
> *desire and the power to do what pleases him.*
> (Philippians 2:13 NLT)

Earlier, I mentioned Mary and Martha, friends of Jesus. As you'll recall, when Jesus came to visit them, Martha busied herself with many things she believed were necessary to properly welcome Jesus as her guest. At the same time, Mary, her sister, sat at Jesus' feet to listen and hear what he had to say. This frustrated Martha. She thought Mary should be helping her.

I can just imagine Martha fuming in the kitchen as she wondered when Mary would get on her feet and help her, so both of them could relax and enjoy Jesus' visit. Finally, Martha couldn't stand it anymore. She demanded that Mary help her. In response, Jesus told her that Mary had made the better choice and that she should not be prevented from listening to him (Luke 10:38-42).

Martha thought her work was important. Jesus was their dearest family friend. She wanted to give him a proper welcome in her home. But Jesus said Mary made the better choice. He made it clear that it's more important to put aside some of our activities, no matter how well intentioned, so we can focus on him. Often, our work or activities are helpful to others, whether in our homes, communities, or churches. But if we aren't focused on God and connected with Jesus, our work will be in vain.

Individually, we cannot do it all. With the daily chores in our homes and our jobs, we are often overwhelmed. Every hour, every day, every week is frequently booked with the obligations of the day. We need help. Just like Martha, we might wonder when Mary is going to start helping us.

Choose the right thing. Align with Christ first, and through him our priorities can be set. When we are aligned with Christ, God will enable us to do more than we could ever imagine.

The harvest is plentiful; the need is great.

How do I know what I can or should do? How do I know that God wants me to do something? Some will respond, "I help at church, I check on my elderly neighbor, and I volunteer at the homeless shelter. These things are important. I don't have time for anything else." Those things *are* important. They might be the exact things God has called you to do. But for some of us, God has a different plan. God calls all of us.

Have you heard his call? Do you question whether the message you're hearing is actually from God?

God doesn't always show up in a burning bush to tell us what he wants us to do, as he did with Moses. But he could.

God doesn't always send an angel to announce his plans as he did with Mary, the mother of Jesus. But he could. We might encounter angels with or without our knowledge.

Sometimes God uses a still small voice, a voice some of us might attribute to our conscience, a broken heart, or a sense of right and wrong. God speaks to us through a thought that awakens us in the night or through a dream. He changes our circumstances, our jobs, our family dynamics, or our circle of friends to enable us to hear his call.

God's call may or may not seem to make sense. Is he calling you to build an ark or move your family to a new location without saying where you are to go? Sometimes God expects you to hear him, accept his call, and trust him to take care of the details.

God does talk to us. He calls to each and every one of us. So we can be workers in and for his kingdom.

The harvest is plentiful. The need is great.

We need to be close enough to God to hear his whisper and feel his nudging. We need to know him well, so that when he calls, we recognize his voice.

Draw close to God through frequent prayer. *Pray continually,* the apostle Paul said (1 Thessalonians 5:17). Seek him through Bible reading, study, and research. Develop your relationship with him through active worship, contemplation of his creation, and quiet time in his presence. Draw close enough to God to hear his voice and feel his warm, moist breath as he whispers in your ear.

> *A hurricane wind ripped through the mountains and shattered the rocks before GOD, but GOD wasn't to be found in the wind; after the wind an earthquake, but GOD wasn't in the earthquake; and after the earthquake fire, but GOD wasn't in the fire; and after the fire a gentle and quiet whisper.* (1 Kings 19:11-12 MSG)

The psalmist said, *Unless the* LORD *builds the house, the builders labor in vain* (Psalm 127:1). Find God. Look around you. What house is God building? Where and with whom is God likely working to impact our world in a positive way? Observe the opportunities that arise. Then step up to the plate, take a swing at the ball, and see where it takes you. Maybe you'll hit a single, a double, or even a home run. Maybe you'll strike out. But when you're working with God, right along by his side, on something that is important to him, you'll get on base. The doubles, triples, and home runs will come when you find yourself working in direct response to God's call to you.

I volunteer from time to time for an organization called Elizabeth Ministry. They are an international movement "designed to offer hope and healing for women and their families on issues related to childbearing, sexuality, and relationships."[3] I like to think of their work as touching all things family. The amount of my involvement tends to ebb and flow. Sometimes I provide legal research. Other times I help with a conference idea or simply through donations. The need seems to shift through time. There have been times when I thought it was time for me to move on, perhaps to support a different organization.

But there's something about Elizabeth Ministry that keeps a grip on me. When I enter the doors, I feel a sense of calm and warmth even on a frantic or cold day. When I speak with their employees, I find a commitment that far exceeds their wages. When I speak to the founder and the other volunteers, I hear and see the love of God. I believe God works through Elizabeth Ministry, and it's God's presence that keeps me from moving on completely.

I connected with them several years ago after a friend sent me an article about them from a local newspaper. She sent the article because she thought their work and my interests were

---

3   Elizabeth Ministry International, *www.elizabethministry.com* (August 27, 2014).

aligned. I didn't know anything about them other than what was in the article, but a sense of curiosity developed as I read and reread the article. After about six months, maybe more, I finally went to the Elizabeth Ministry resource center to see what they had to offer. I didn't see anything I needed or wanted that day, but my curiosity continued to draw me back to them. Finally, after a few visits to the resource center over a period of a few months, I met with the founder to learn more about them. After our conversation, I knew I wanted to get involved in some manner. I wasn't sure what I might do or what my involvement might entail. But God was there and his presence pulled on me like a magnet.

> *"I am the vine; you are the branches. If you remain*
> *in me and I in you, you will bear much fruit; apart*
> *from me you can do nothing."* (John 15:5)

Opportunities to find where God is working are all around us. Sometimes they're presented by a friend, a newspaper article, a notice on a bulletin board, or a simple sign on the face of a building. In some cases, they're obvious. Often, they're simply within our daily circumstances, as with Esther. She found herself in King Xerxes' harem. After becoming his queen, she was in a position to save her people, the Jews, from certain destruction.

When I first approached Elizabeth Ministry, I was cautious and not immediately sure it was a ministry I wanted to support. Being cautious resulted in a short delay in my opportunity to work alongside God and support Elizabeth Ministry. Fortunately for me, the short delay caused no harm in this case.

Sometimes it's important to discern whether a particular opportunity is a call from God. The question we must ask is, "Am I doing what I can *with* I AM?" On the other hand, some delays in action might result in missed opportunities. Some circumstances require us to do something *right now*.

Once, as I stood in line at the grocery store on the afternoon of Christmas Eve with the last items I needed for our evening dinner, I noticed the man in front of me. He was buying two frozen pizzas. My thoughts dipped into the recesses of my personal Christmas memories, back to the year I had no plans for Christmas and spent Christmas Eve alone. That year, I stood in line at the grocery store just like this man and waited to pay for a frozen pizza for my Christmas Eve meal. I observed the man as the store clerk wished him a Merry Christmas. He responded gruffly. He clearly didn't anticipate having a merry Christmas.

My mind raced. *Should I say something? Should I invite him to our house for dinner? He's a stranger. That's not a safe choice. Perhaps I could invite him to join our family at a restaurant. What restaurant is open on Christmas Eve? What time did we plan to go to church? I could invite him to church. What should I say? What should I ....?*

In a moment, he was out the door. I missed the opportunity to offer Christmas cheer and exhibit the love of Christ. I missed the opportunity to do what I could, where I was. I believe God was calling me to step up to the plate and offer an invitation. I didn't join God in this critical moment and missed my chance to show this man God's love on Christmas Eve.

Jesus said he is the Vine and we are the branches. With him we will bear much fruit and make a difference. If we remain in him, we can be the somebody who does something. In him, we can make a difference. We don't have to do it alone. In fact, we can't do it alone. It's best if we do what we can with I AM, with God, and with Christ.

I will do what I can, where I am, with I AM. What will you do?

I Will Do What I Can, Where I Am, With I AM!

Chapter 18

Team Up

"I don't need God in order to be a good person or to do good things," many have said. "I don't need any help. I can just do it myself."

I suppose you could do it yourself, depending on what it is you're trying to do. Independence and the desire for personal accomplishment internally drive many of us, as inherent attributes. If you've ever taken care of a young child for any length of time, you've probably heard these words: "Let me do it. I want to do it myself!" Then, whether the child was capable or not, he gave it a try under your watchful eye. If the child was successful, you likely gave him praise. If the child wasn't successful, you probably provided some help and gave further instruction, guidance, and encouragement.

When we struggle to do it alone, whatever *it* may be, God is the loving caretaker, our heavenly Father. He stands beside us, keeps a watchful eye, and steps in when we seek his help.

> *I will instruct you and teach you in the way you*
> *should go; I will counsel you with my loving eye on*
> *you.* (Psalm 32:8)

My husband is an extremely helpful person. So much so, that I occasionally want to say, "Let me do it. I want to do it myself." I try not to say that, of course. I'm afraid that if I say I want to do it myself, he'll let me do it myself. Frankly, I truly appreciate his help and never want to discourage him.

I remember when I painted our barn a few years ago. I don't mean that I painted a barn on canvas. I painted our 100-year-old, two-story, grayish-red barn with rotted white trim, precariously hanging doors, and a metal roof. It desperately needed paint and repair after years of neglect. I had four ladders, the smallest being a five-foot stepladder and the largest being a forty-foot extension ladder. I used the largest ladder only when my husband was home because it was too heavy for me to move and set up by myself. However, on this particular day, Wayne was at work, and I didn't want the painting to wait for the weekend. *I can do it myself*, I thought. *I can maneuver the ladder. It's heavy, but if I use leverage, I'm sure I can do it.*

We stored the ladder inside the barn, along the wall in the haymow, a large room with a dirt floor covered in a bed of loose hay of varying depths. As I moved the long and heavy ladder from its resting place, intending to tip it onto its side, the foot of the ladder caught in the hay, and caused me to lose my grip. Down it fell. The cold, hard metal hit my head on its way to the ground.

I discovered two things. One, if I get hit on the head just right with a heavy object, I will see stars just like those depicted as spinning around a cartoon character's head. Two, it's wise to recognize and appreciate your limits and get help as needed. Doing it alone isn't always best or even possible.

When we respond to God's call on our lives, we never need to do it alone.

"Ask and it will be given to you; seek and you will

*find; knock and the door will be opened to you. For
everyone who asks receives; the one who seeks finds;
and to the one who knocks, the door will be opened."*
(Matthew 7:7-8)

Remember Moses and his discussion with God at the burning bush?

God said, "Go."

Moses said, "Who me? I'm not qualified. I can't do it. I need help."

God said, "I'll give you all the help you need."

Yet Moses didn't think he could do it. Moses wanted God to send someone else. God got angry with Moses because of his reluctance and lack of faith in God's promise to help. Trust God. When you're doing what you can in an affirmative response to God's call, God will enable you. He'll help and give you all that you need.

I can do all this through him who gives me strength.
(Philippians 4:13)

I will do what I can, where I am, with I AM. He will enable me, strengthen me, and be with me. With God, we can do all things according to his will.

When I was in school, oh so many years ago, personal effort, rather than teamwork, was expected. Administrators designed schoolwork with the idea that each person would work alone. To work with classmates was viewed as cheating, depending on the degree of help that was offered to each other. Now team effort is applauded, encouraged, and often required. Working together enables each person to contribute their specific knowledge or skill that others on the team may not have. This teamwork results in a better project result. Teams work best when each member's skills and abilities complement, rather than duplicate, those of the other team members.

This is not a new concept. It is clear from biblical teachings that each of us has different abilities, and God expects us to work together, as a team, to form a single body. *For just as each of us has one body with many members, and these members do not all have the same function, so in Christ we, though many, form one body, and each member belongs to all the others. We have different gifts, according to the grace given to each of us. If your gift is prophesying, then prophesy in accordance with your faith; if it is serving, then serve; if it is teaching, then teach; if it is to encourage, then give encouragement; if it is giving, then give generously; if it is to lead, do it diligently; if it is to show mercy, do it cheerfully* (Romans 12:4-8).

We are to do what we can according to our abilities and gifts, working along with our brothers and sisters in Christ. If we do it alone, the result might be less than it could be.

When we work with our brothers and sisters in Christ, it creates renewed energy like a relay team at a track meet. Each runner only runs part of the entire race. The first runner hands the baton to the next runner, who continues the race with a fresh pace until it's time to pass the baton on to the next runner, who ultimately hands it off to the fourth runner. As a result, the four runners complete a sixteen-hundred-meter race significantly faster than a single runner who runs the distance alone. By working together, with our brothers and sisters in Christ and with God himself, we can accomplish great things.

> *Let us think of ways to motivate one another to acts of love and good works. And let us not neglect our meeting together, as some people do, but encourage one another, especially now that the day of his return is drawing near.* (Hebrews 10:24-25 NLT)

Teamwork doesn't come naturally for me. I find it very difficult to ask someone for help. I don't want to impose, and

4:8). If we keep our focus on what is good, noble, admirable, excellent, and praiseworthy, we will find it easier to exercise patience, control our tempers, and work as a team to make the positive change intended by the effort.

We can do so much more if we join God and join our brothers and sisters in Christ. God's team is the winning team. Without God and other helpers, the ladder will tumble down, and we will do nothing but see stars. The race will be too long, and our legs will get too heavy to keep going. Just as with a new runner on the relay team, God and his team add zeal, energy, and ability.

> *Do you not know? Have you not heard? The LORD is the everlasting God, the Creator of the ends of the earth. He will not grow tired or weary, and his understanding no one can fathom. He gives strength to the weary and increases the power of the weak.* (Isaiah 40:28-29)

I will do what I can, where I am, with I AM ... and with my brothers and sisters in Christ, and (I hope) with you as well.

I Will Do What I Can, Where I Am, With I AM!

Chapter 19

Just Say Yes!

Whatever is good and perfect is a gift coming down
to us from God our Father, who created all the lights

While I watched a church service on television recently, the pastor[4] noted milestones impacting the general mindset of the Israelites of the Old Testament. He described the first mindset held by the Israelites to be that of slaves during the 430 years they lived in Egypt.

The second mindset of the Israelites was that of children of God. The Israelites had this mindset during the forty years they wandered in the wilderness. They were no longer in Egypt but were not yet in the Promised Land. During this period, God provided everything for the Israelites, including food (manna and quail), water, clothing that didn't wear out, and daily guidance as to their travel instructions. God also used their time in the wilderness to strengthen their trust and faith in him, to teach them about obedience, and to discipline them when they failed to act obediently. God provided for the Israelites just as a good parent provides for a child.

Whatever is good and perfect is a gift coming down
to us from God our Father, who created all the lights

---

4   Jentezen Franklin.

*in the heavens. He never changes or casts a shifting
shadow.* (James 1:17 NLT)

After forty years in the wilderness, the Israelites had to
develop the mindset of soldiers in order to move into the
Promised Land and defeat those who already inhabited the
territory and cities. In God's time and with his strength and
backing, the Israelites crossed over the Jordan River and engaged
the enemies of God in battle.

As I heard the pastor's description of the three primary
mindsets of the Israelites, I had a break-through moment and
exclaimed to myself, *That's me! That explains everything!*

The description of the Israelites' changing mindsets not only
described where I've been spiritually, but it also explained why
I sense this new urgency to do what I can, where I am, with I
AM. It explains my newfound interest in community, national,
and world affairs. His description of Israel's mindsets helps me
understand my disheartenment over the continual decline in
moral behavior and foundational grounding in faith in the
United States. And it provides me with motivation to pursue
my ever-increasing desire to make a positive difference in the
lives of others, in our world today, and for God's kingdom.

In my early years, I lived as a slave to sin just as the Israelites
were slaves in Egypt. When I accepted Jesus Christ as my
Savior, I began to live as a child of God. I basked comfortably
in his provision, knowing that he loved me as his child, forgave my sins, and would always be there to give me strength
in all circumstances, whether good or bad. Now I hold a deep
concern for what's happening in the world around me. I try to
do what's right and good and feel true remorse when I realize
my mistakes and failures. My heart breaks when I see those I
love choose to walk apart from God. I've discovered that life
isn't about me. It's about God and his kingdom.

*Jesus Christ is the same yesterday and today and
forever.* (Hebrews 13:8)

God doesn't change. What he did in the lives of the Israelites,
to impact and change their mindsets over time, he will do again
in each of our lives. We have all been slaves to sin. Many of
us have accepted Jesus as our Savior and know the love of our
Father God in our daily lives. Some of us enjoy this position
as a child of God so much that we choose to remain where we
are, because we feel at peace. We desire to simply learn more,
worship him daily, and spend prayerful time in his presence.
But God wants us to do more. He wants us to get off of our
loveseat, out of our cozy parlors, and into the world. He wants
us to live out his love in our relationships with others and in
all that we do. He wants us to love out loud.

At some point, sometimes for just a moment and sometimes
for the rest of our lives, God calls us to action. He calls us to
become soldiers for his kingdom.

Jesus prayed for unity. It was his dying wish, his last will and
testament for all people. Through unity with Christ, we will not
only live in God's love but also share his love with all whom
we encounter and in all that we do. By doing so, all people will
know that Jesus is God's son, the Messiah.

Through unity with Christ, we will be able to do the
unimaginable. Like the apostle Paul, we will be able to do *all
things* through Christ, as he will strengthen us. In unity with
Jesus, we *will* bear much fruit, just as Jesus promised when he
said that he is the Vine and we are the branches. This is a guar-
antee. *With Jesus*, as we live and work in unity with him, we
can do all things according to God's plan. We will be soldiers
in the army of God.

You might wonder whether I've found the words of this
book to ring true in my life. The answer is an emphatic "Yes!"

God has been working on my heart to increase my attentiveness to the world around me. For reasons I didn't understand until now, God created in me an interest in national and world affairs. I've become a news junkie. I watch the news, read the news, and talk about the news. In particular, I find myself keenly interested in the impact of our state and federal governmental leaders' politically motivated decisions on our lives and on the long-term financial stability and security of our nation. I find myself genuinely concerned about the moral decline of our society, the breakdown of the traditional family, and the forced removal of God from all things public. And I fear that the average citizen of the United States has become so self-focused, causing such divisiveness, that the latter half of the saying, "United we stand, divided we fall," predicts our nation's future.

As I watch the news, my heart breaks, and I wonder what I can do. When I discuss current events with family, friends, and members of my Bible study group, all people say the same thing, "What can we do?"

Previously, as I sat comfortably in my role as a child of God on my loveseat and in my parlor, I would respond to that question with, "Somebody should do something." Now I respond with, "We can do something. With God, the Great I AM, we can do something."

It might be a small start, but I wrote my first-ever letter to the editor of our local newspaper. I don't like conflict. So, up until recently, I've been afraid to publicly take any stand that might stir up angry or argumentative responses. Yet rather than back away from topics that might be controversial, God blessed me with the courage to voice my opinion in conversations, in my writings, and in social media. I've found the courage to stop using two business cards, a Christian card and a secular card.

Why am I hiding my faith in my business dealings? I wondered. I now use a single business card with my faith clearly represented.

These might sound like baby steps to you, and maybe they are. But they were big steps for me. I had to start somewhere doing what I can, where I am, with I AM.

God has since called me to help my mother. At eighty-eight years old, she was the passenger in a car when it was struck by another car at an intersection and rolled over. She suffered several broken bones, including a broken neck. Now, over a year later, her injuries have healed pretty well, although she faces some residual issues. She has moved to an assisted living facility. This accident not only changed her life permanently, but also changed my life instantly. I had to step in as one of her two primary caregivers. The job is exhausting, but God is there to help. He's been a visible force from the moment of the accident. In my mom's case, I can, with I AM, make a difference.

Are you ready to make a difference? Are you ready to become the somebody who steps up to the plate and does something? With the Great I AM, you can make a difference.

I will do what I can, where I am, with I AM. Has this sentence of commitment taken root in your heart?

The harvest is plentiful. The workers are few. There is much to do. Somebody needs to do something. Do you want to be that somebody?

People are hurting and suffering. There are new and deadly diseases. Our neighborhoods, communities, states, and nations are struggling. Our social culture and moral fabric are declining. There is unrest, war, and political upheaval throughout the entire world. Christians are being persecuted worldwide, even in our dear United States. There are many people who don't know God, many who don't know Jesus, and many who haven't yet been blessed by the Holy Spirit. Somebody should do something.

With I AM, each of us can make a difference. Together we can change this world. We just need to say, "Here I am, Lord. I want the job. I'm ready to be a soldier in your army. With you, Lord, I can do it. Just show me the way."

Together, we can, with I AM, make a difference!

Are you ready to commit to do what you can with the Great I AM?

I Will Do What I Can, Where I Am, With I AM!

Chapter 20

Get Started

Trust in the LORD and do good. Then you will live safely in the land and prosper. Take delight in the LORD, and he will give you your heart's desires.

Commit everything you do to the LORD. Trust him, and he will help you. He will make your innocence radiate like the dawn, and the justice of your cause will shine like the noonday sun. (Psalm 37:3-6 NLT)

I'm willing. Where do I start? I want to do what I can, where I am, with I AM.

What breaks your heart? What causes you to worry? What makes you exclaim, "Somebody should do something!" Now is your chance to be that somebody.

Maybe your heart bleeds for one of the following:

- Orphans
- Abused children
- Children in foster care
- Elder abuse

- Elder care
- Lack of respect for mature adults
- Young girls with an inactive father figure
- Young boys with insufficient role models
- Teen pregnancy
- Declining moral values in our children and society
- Increasing crime
- Apathy of our youth
- Disrespect for human life
- Ineffective government
- ISIS, Al Qaeda, or other terrorist groups
- Persecution of Christians
- Persecution of Jews
- Sex trafficking
- Modern-day slave trading
- Excessive government
- The homeless
- The unemployed or underemployed
- Economic security of our country
- Security of our country locally and internationally
- Threat of war
- International poverty and hunger
- Local poverty and hunger
- Ineffective schools and education systems
- The decline of the traditional family
- The increasing divorce rate
- Disease control and cures

- Clean water supplies
- Declining church influence
- Non-biblical church teachings
- Lack of protection for the lives of our preborn infants
- Alcohol or drug use and abuse
- Racial divides
- Aid for the mentally ill
- Support for the physically or mentally challenged
- Animal abuse
- Safe food supplies
- Gangs
- Inadequate or unavailable health care
- Quality support for our veterans

Look how long this list is! Yet I've only scratched the surface. Perhaps I missed something that's on your heart. Add it to the list.

Somebody should do something!

I am somebody. You are somebody. Together we are somebody. Together with God, the Great I AM, we can do something. In unity with Jesus, we can do something. As Jesus said, *"I am the vine; you are the branches. If you remain in me and I in you, you **will** bear much fruit; apart from me you can do nothing"* (John 15:5, emphasis added).

We start with Jesus. Spend time with him in prayer. If there's a cause or issue that's on your heart, tell him in prayer that you want to do something. Ask him in prayer to show you what to do. Tell him in prayer that you want to do what you can with him. We know we'll bear much fruit and that all things are possible in Christ. Pray daily about the cause that's on your heart.

Then, listen for his call. Watch for open doors and

opportunities. Research the issue on the Internet, through your local library, and your church home. Search out others with the same concern. There are likely many charitable organizations who already try to serve this need, and they would likely welcome your support in either time or money. Your church leaders might encourage you to start something in or through the church. It's even possible that your pastor will invite you to take charge and see where your idea goes. However, don't feel dejected or angry if church leaders or pastors don't embrace your idea. Continue to pray and seek God's guidance.

I can do all this through him who gives me strength.
(Philippians 4:13)

Maybe you want to increase the passion for one or more of these issues in the hearts of others within your circle of friends, in your neighborhood, in your church, in your community, or in your dorm, college, or school. Consider starting an "I Can with I AM" discussion group or an "I Can with I AM" coffee group.

Increase each participant's understanding of the issues. Bring in local representatives of charitable organizations and service organizations to speak to your group and raise awareness for their work and the people they serve. Share information from the news.

Discuss the issues openly and respectfully, but be aware that people may have differing opinions on the issues. Seek biblical guidance on the issues through direct research of the Bible, consultation with your church pastor, and by reading and discussing Christian books on the topic.

The goal of an "I Can with I AM" group is to spawn interest and action. Discussions should include brainstorming sessions about what someone might do. However, remember that not everyone in the group will be interested in the same issue. No one should be made to feel that they must support the issue being discussed. God may call them in a different direction, and that's the direction they should be encouraged to go. In all "I Can with I AM" groups, remind participants that they shouldn't feel pressured to volunteer or otherwise support the issue being discussed. Emphasize that their active discussion in the group is enough unless God puts it on their hearts to take further action.

Perhaps you don't have time for a "I Can with I AM" group. Maybe you love social media or like to blog. Consider ways you might influence your connections or friends to take action through social media. Increase their awareness by sharing information from the news or about your favorite charitable organization.

It's time to get started. I am somebody. You are somebody. Together we are somebody. Together, in unity with Christ, we can do it. We can make a difference. We will bear much fruit.

I can with I AM!

I Will Do What I Can, Where I Am, With I AM!

Connect with Sheila

Online: www.Sheilaluck.com

Facebook: www.facebook.com/sheilamluck

Meet the Author

Sheila Luck has worked as an engineer, attorney and mediator. Her goal is to help others pursue their God-given potential through her books, blogs, and speaking events. Always using a biblical and personal approach, Sheila has provided inspiration, motivation and direction to women, young adults and students for over 10 years. Her uplifting, motivational, yet heartfelt messages help others become the "somebody" that God intended them to be, giving them the courage to act.

Other Titles by

Sheila M. Luck

We were told it would be easy. We thought it was the best choice; but now we suffer with the consequences, the regular reminders, a sense of guilt, and a sense of shame. Through abortion, we now face the death of our babies, death by choice. We try to hide our choice and we try to escape the emotional pain. We seek forgiveness, acceptance, and consolation; yet, we find no solace. Our fears drive us into a life of secrecy, hiding our loss. We suffer a secret loss.

My Secret Loss will:

- Enable the reader to accept the truth about abortion

- Provide permission and encouragement to grieve the loss of your baby

- Validate your emotional and psychological harm that has been caused by abortion

- Discover the path to peace, healing that is only possible through the saving grace of Jesus

Available where books are sold

Choice, Death, and the Aftermath

Fearfully and desperately wanting to hide my mistakes and deny the unwanted, but not totally unexpected ramifications of my earlier choices, I chose what seemed to be the easiest answer. I chose death, and then I moved into the aftermath of my choice. I, for a lifetime and beyond, will live in the aftermath of my choice. Although there is recovery, through forgiveness, there are lasting ramifications. No one told me that the ramifications of my choice would last forever. No one told me what my choice would do to my heart. No one told me that my choice was, in fact, a death sentence for my baby.

This book is for:

- Moms wrestling with choice and an unplanned teen pregnancy

- Loved ones who are seeking resolution after abortion

- Anyone who has had an abortion and wants to know how to feel better.

Available where books are sold

For I know the plans I have for you," declares the Lord, "plans to prosper you and not to harm you, plans to give you hope and a future (Jeremiah 29:11, NIV).

Losing your job creates a new opportunity to discover God's plans for your future. This is great news. Not because you will land that dream job, but because you will discover God's will for your life, and by doing so you will sense genuine fulfillment as He fulfills His plans through you.

This book helps you:

- Identify and define your God-given career and life story.

- Set parameters for a strong, focused job search.

- Become armed with clear employment guidelines.

- Start out your new career on the right foot (or rejuvenate your existing job).

Available where books are sold

Other Titles by

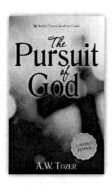

To have found God and still to pursue Him is a paradox of love, scorned indeed by the too-easily-satisfied religious person, but justified in happy experience by the children of the burning heart. Saint Bernard of Clairvaux stated this holy paradox in a musical four-line poem that will be instantly understood by every worshipping soul:

> *We taste Thee, O Thou Living Bread,*
> *And long to feast upon Thee still:*
> *We drink of Thee, the Fountainhead*
> *And thirst our souls from Thee to fill.*

Come near to the holy men and women of the past and you will soon feel the heat of their desire after God. Let A. W. Tozer's pursuit of God spur you also into a genuine hunger and thirst to truly know God.

Overcome your greatest enemy, yourself.

Are you an overcomer? Or, are you plagued by little sins that easily beset you? Even worse, are you failing in your Christian walk, but refuse to admit and address it? No Christian can afford to dismiss the call to be an overcomer. The earthly cost is minor; the eternal reward is beyond measure.

Dwight L. Moody is a master at unearthing what ails us. He uses stories and humor to bring to light the essential principles of successful Christian living. Each aspect of overcoming is looked at from a practical and understandable angle. The solution Moody presents for our problems is not religion, rules, or other outward corrections. Instead, he takes us to the heart of the matter and prescribes biblical, God-given remedies for every Christian's life. Get ready to embrace genuine victory for today, and joy for eternity.

Available where books are sold

Why are many Christians often defeated? Because they pray so little. Why do most men see so few brought *out of darkness to light* by their ministry? Because they pray so little. Why are our churches simply not on fire for God? Because there is so little real prayer.

We may be assured of this: The secret of all failure is our failure in secret prayer.

This book explores, in depth:

- God's wonder at our lack of prayer
- God's incredible promises concerning those who do pray
- God's condition for providing signs
- God's desire for earnest prayer
- God's perspective on hindrances to prayer

Lord Jesus is as powerful today as ever before. The Lord Jesus is as anxious for men to be saved as ever before. His arm is not shortened that it cannot save, but He does stretch forth His arm unless we pray more – and more genuinely. Prayer, real prayer, is the noblest, the sublimest and most stupendous act that any creature of God can perform. Lord, teach us how to pray.

Available where books are sold